Ancient Egyptian Literature

ANCIENT
Egyptian Literature

An Anthology

TRANSLATED BY JOHN L. FOSTER

UNIVERSITY OF TEXAS PRESS

This book has been supported by an endowment dedicated to classics and the ancient world, funded by grants from the National Endowment for the Humanities
and the Gladys Krieble Delmas Foundation, the James R. Dougherty, Jr., Foundation, and the Rachael and Ben Vaughan Foundation, and by gifts from Mark and Jo
Ann Finley, Lucy Shoe Meritt, Anne Byrd Nalle, and other individual donors.

"Why, just now, must you question your heart"; "I love you through the daytimes";
"My love is one and only"; "Love, how I'd love to slip down to the pond"; "Love of
you is mixed deep in my vitals"; "I think I'll go home and lie very still"; and songs
i–viii from Songs of the Birdcatcher's Daughter originally appeared in *Love Songs of
the New Kingdom,* by John L. Foster, reprinted by the University of Texas Press,
Austin, 1992. Used here with permission.

   Prayer to the King to Rise Up; Hymn to the King as a Primordial God; Hymn
to the King as a Flash of Lightning; Prayer of the King as a Star Fading in the
Dawn; The Greatness of the King; Prayer of King Ramesses II; Hymn to the Rising Sun; In Praise of Amun; The Prayers of Pahery; From the Tomb of King Intef
first appeared in *Hymns, Prayers, and Songs: An Anthology of Ancient Egyptian Lyric
Poetry* (SBL Writings from the Ancient World 8) Atlanta: Scholars Press, 1995.
Used here with permission.

Requests for permission to reproduce material from this work should be sent to
Permissions, University of Texas Press, P.O. Box 7819, Austin, TX 78713-7819.

♾ The paper used in this book meets the minimum requirements of ANSI/NISO
Z39.48-1992 (R1997) (Permanence of Paper).

Library of Congress Cataloging-in-Publication Data

Ancient Egyptian literature : an anthology / translated by John L. Foster.
      p.   cm.
   Includes bibliographical references.
   ISBN 0-292-72527-2 (pbk. : alk. paper)
      1. Egyptian literature—Translations into English.   I. Foster, John L. (John
Lawrence), 1930–
PJ1943 .A53   2001
893'.108—dc21   00-061607

To my friends

and colleagues

at the

Oriental Institute,

University of Chicago

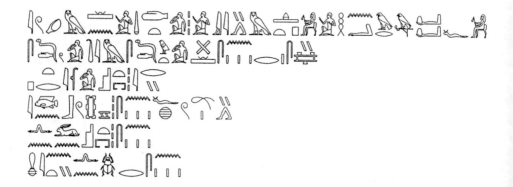

I have heard the words of Imhotep, and Hordjedef, too,

retold time and again in their narrations.

Where are their dwellings now?

Their walls are down,

Their places gone,

like something that has never been.

Harper's Song from the Tomb of King Intef

CONTENTS

PREFACE

i

The following pieces are gathered from earlier volumes of my translations of ancient Egyptian literature: the entirety of *Echoes of Egyptian Voices* (1992), and selections from *Love Songs of the New Kingdom* (1974; 1992) and *Hymns, Prayers, and Songs: An Anthology of Ancient Egyptian Lyric Poetry* (1995). In addition, there are four longer poems: *The Instruction for Little Pepi, The Prophecy of Neferty, The Instruction for Merikarê,* and *The Wisdom of Amenemopet,* as well as two new shorter poems. The result is a representative selection of ancient Egyptian literature.

All this began when, as a graduate student at the University of Michigan, I came across a translation of a Harper's Song from ancient Egypt hung on the wall above a sarcophagus in the hallway of the Kelsey Museum. The words struck me as surprisingly lively coming from a civilization that was so in love with death (the usual misinterpretation). I finished my work in American literature and modern poetry and went on to a teaching career in English. But I pursued the interest engendered by that Harper's Song, did post-doctoral study at the Oriental Institute of the University of Chicago, and for the past thirty-five years have worked at translating ancient Egyptian literature into English in a way that treats the pieces as poems while attempting to preserve their fidelity to the original language.

ii

The two great hindrances to any proper appreciation of the literature and civilization of ancient Egypt are the Bible and the glory that was Greece. These two sources—and the civilizations that produced them—are the twin bastions of our Western culture; and since they have so undeniably formed us and the very ways we think, it is no wonder we approach other cultures in terms of what they have taught us. Our view of ancient history is conditioned by what we understand as true from ancient Greece and, particularly, Israel. Indeed, our very idea of what constitutes ancient history is filtered through the accounts of Genesis and Exodus.

What has happened to Egyptology in the century and a half since Champollion deciphered the hieroglyphs, back at a time when one studied ancient Egypt only for confirmation of biblical attitudes? The difference has been the partial recovery, during the past 150 years, of the languages, histories, and cultures of the high civilizations of the ancient Near East; and these enable us to study and understand a country like Egypt from its own documents and monuments and from its own point of view. This increased knowledge has demonstrated that the version of ancient history that we have been brought to know and cherish has been a very much oversimplified and parochial one, projecting the viewpoint, at the earliest, of an ancient Israelite author who wrote during the united monarchy, some time later than 1000 B.C.

Egyptian writing, on the other hand, began some *two millennia* earlier, around 3000 B.C.; and civilization had been proceeding in high gear over the entire Fertile Crescent for at least that same two-thousand-year period before King David. We need to realize that some forty percent — *almost half* — of recorded human history occurred before King David. The selections in this volume are all from that earlier time, some of them from the earliest time, composed toward the dawn of writing, of literature, and of history itself.

Because of our classical-Christian value system we have traditionally accepted the biblical account of ancient history as true and tried to fit evidence from extra-biblical sources into that system. This no longer works. Notice that the classical authorities, those upon whom the earliest students of ancient Egypt relied — Herodotus, Diodorus Siculus, and Strabo — lived and wrote even later than the Yahwist and Elohist of Israelite tradition. Herodotus lived during the fifth century B.C., and the other two were both first-century figures. Even Manetho, from whom we take our division of Egyptian dynasties, only lived as far back as the third century B.C. Such writers — classical and Israelite alike — knew an Egypt that was but a shadow of its former self, that had long since ceded its greatness to later, more youthful empires.

There is another consequence of this unfortunate earlier perspective. Because we in the West have valued the contributions of the ancient Greeks and Hebrews as fundamental to our very being, we have lovingly preserved whatever was written in both languages. Not too long ago a university education centered on a study of the Greek and Roman classics and was often augmented by the study of Hebrew. The result has been over two millennia of careful attention to these ancient texts: the Hebrew because they were the sacred Word of God, and the Greek because they were the fountainhead of our Western literature and philosophy. Because of this high valuation, there has developed over the centuries a rich tradition of translating these relics of our origins. Translators can turn to the past to weigh how a passage was understood by many kindred spirits over time; and this slow process has improved and polished the results.

Now let us turn to the case of Egypt. Egyptian hieroglyphic is a dead language. Its meaning only began to be recovered when Champollion deciphered the hieroglyphs in 1822. And it was not until the last quarter of the nineteenth century that a tradition of translating the hieroglyphs into English could even begin to develop. Translation of ancient Egyptian literature is barely a century old, only four or five generations of Egyptologists have had a chance to work on the language, and most of the effort has of necessity been devoted to basics—vocabulary, word order, and sentence patterns. These efforts of earlier language scholars have been absolutely fundamental to, and necessarily preceded, any attempt to recover ancient Egyptian literature *as literature* and *as poetry.*

Our cultural traditions, along with loss of the key to the hieroglyphic language for so many centuries, have blinded us to the value of what has survived from the literature of ancient Egypt. It has riches thus far largely unrealized.

iii

When one considers ancient Egypt, the first images that come to mind are of the pyramids at Giza, or the Sphinx, or the dried mummies in their coffins, or the consummate gold work of the treasure of Tutankhamun, or the huge statues of Ramesses II. Egypt, indeed, was one of the first lights of civilization, and these images remind us of that fact. When we ponder its surviving buildings and monuments, its carvings and paintings, its gold work and jewelry, its statues and figurines, we cannot help but be impressed by the primacy of ancient Egyptian culture. These survivals guarantee the perennial fascination the world has with that ancient civilization. And as we look into the faces of Egyptian statues and figurines—which are usually generic and idealized, but lifelike—we wonder what went on in the minds of their owners, in the minds of those Egyptians the statues and figurines were meant to embody. We ask what went on behind such eyes. What world did they see? What gave those faces their expressions?

Indeed, one wonders what a society that could create such excellence in architecture, in painting, in precious metal and stone, and in statuary—what did, or could, it similarly create in words? What Mind stood behind those hands that created the visual masterpieces of ancient Egypt? And how did that Mind express itself verbally? As one first trained in English and American literature, I have been intrigued by this aspect of Egyptian civilization for over thirty-five years. And I would argue that the splendor of pharaonic visual art has its worthy parallel in Egyptian literature: it is indeed a full-blooded verbal equivalent to the richness, elegance, vitality, and variety of Egypt's visual remains. Egyptians honored the Word as it became flesh in hymns and prayers, instructions, stories, and even love songs; and Egyptian writers—the poets particularly—delighted in working (or playing) with the nuances of words and meaning, and in the sounds and images of the language.

Yet the works of ancient Egyptian literature and their authors are less well known than the works of art and architecture. This is partly due to problems in deciphering the details of the language and partly due to the condition of the surviving texts. But it also stems from the fact that the nonspecialist must *read* the literature, not merely see a slide of Egypt or view it on a tour. And in trying to read, he or she must also try to visualize the images and culture conveyed in the text—which is no easy thing to do. At any rate, far from appearing in their rightful place at the fountainhead of world literature, the classics of Egypt remain out of the mainstream, covered in darkness.

What can be said about that literature? First of all, the Egyptian language is old and venerable—known from the beginning of dynastic history (ca. 3100 B.C.) and lasting until the fourth century A.D., when the last hieroglyphic inscription was carved on the walls of the temple at Philae. By the time commemorative titles and tomb biographies became widespread during the Old Kingdom, we can see that a long history of hieroglyphic writing had preceded them. Hieroglyphic signs at Saqqara from the tomb of King Djoser in the Third Dynasty (ca. 2645 B.C.) already show the language in almost classic form. The ancient Egyptian language, then — from the unread earliest signs, through Old, Middle, and Late Egyptian, and on through Demotic and Coptic — had a documented career of almost 3,500 years. By contrast, English — as we can read it without too much aid — has so far survived for only 500 years (that is, back to Chaucer) and spans at best a thousand years, if we go back to Anglo-Saxon, which must be studied as a foreign language.

In addition to this long tradition of written Egyptian, it is important to realize we have physical evidence from these very ancient historical periods: there are pot marks, incised kings' names, and inscriptions carved in stone, wood, and ivory, going back to the very earliest dynasties; papyri (which are extremely fragile) still survive, generally in fragments, some from the Old Kingdom; and ostraca (stones or potsherds with writing or drawing on them) are numerous from the New Kingdom and later. Egyptian literature is known to us, let us say, from *originals*. The text may not have been the author's hand copy, but it does originate from the time when pharaonic Egypt was still vital, and often dates to the period in which the author wrote. We need not rely — as is the case, for instance, in biblical studies — on traditions only later written down or on several centuries of oral transmission.

During the past two decades much has been learned about the nature of Egyptian literature. It was known all along that, as with the literatures of other ancient cultures, the literature of Egypt was almost exclusively religious. Ancient peoples seemed not to have atheism, agnosticism, or skepticism as options in the constellation of their beliefs. But it has now become apparent that ancient Egyptian literature is also almost entirely a verse literature. Very few of the compositions that we would term "literary" (i.e., *belles lettres*) were written in prose — perhaps some of the New Kingdom stories, at best. Rather, all the primary genres — the didactic or "wisdom" texts (instructions, admonitions, and laments), the hymns and prayers, and most of the tales (fiction and myths) — were composed in verse.

The nature of this verse—the style of ancient Egyptian poetry—has also become clearer in recent years. For their poems ancient Egyptian poets used a couplet form: the lines of the poems were grouped in twos, and each pair of lines completed a verse sentence. There were variations upon this basic form (triplets and quatrains), but the generalization is fundamental to understanding the structure of the poems. The verse line was clausal and syntactic: each line consisted of either a dependent or an independent clause; and the pair made up the full sentence. As I said before, the Egyptian poet loved to savor and play with words, since he so respected eloquence and fine language. All the devices of major poetry were employed to enhance the poem: nuances in the vocabulary (connotations of words); imagery (the special images of the Nile Valley, of nature there, and of the special crafts, occupations, professions, and recreations of the people); figurative language (similes and metaphors occurred regularly to enrich meaning); and sound repetition (which was pervasive—for the Egyptian poet richness of sound harmonies was as important as collocations of ideas and images and symbols). In fact, ancient Egyptian poetry was most emphatically *not* a folk poetry (composed by splendidly intuitive untaught artists) but a sophisticated, artful court and temple poetry composed by authors skilled in a long tradition of the craft. The love of words was enriched by a similar love of all the devices used to enhance meaning and effect.

The major remaining gap in our knowledge of ancient Egyptian poetics concerns prosody. The ancient Egyptians did not write the vowels of their words; and since the language died out, these so far are lost to us: we cannot for certain pronounce the language, even though we can understand and translate it. Because of the lack of vowels, and thus pronunciation, we are unable to scan the Egyptian verse line—we do not know for sure if it was composed of feet or if it employed some freer means of determining accents and stresses. I would suggest the verse line was analogous to the free verse of Walt Whitman or the modernist American poets. In fact, I think the stylistic texture or flavor of ancient Egyptian poetry can best be described as a fusion of the free-verse rhythms of those poets just mentioned with the rhetorical and structural regularities—the strict attention to patterns of likeness and difference—of Alexander Pope's eighteenth-century heroic couplets (without the end-rhyme or meter). This combination of stylistic and structural qualities I have termed the "thought couplet"; and the following selections are translated with that style and structure of Egyptian poetry in mind.

iv

The wonder, however, is that we have any ancient Egyptian literature at all. The surfaces upon which the author wrote had to physically survive the ravages of time, enduring from two to five thousand years. We are fortunate in two ways: many compositions were written on stone or pottery (which lasts better than, for instance, human bones); and the hot, dry climate of Egypt helps to preserve not only bones and other perishable objects but papyrus as well, upon which many of the more valued texts were copied to keep them for their own day.

Even so, much of ancient Egyptian literature is a matter of bits and tatters: ragged papyri with holes in them, crumbling into dust when handled; or splinters of stone and bits of pottery containing irritating and tantalizing fragments of text—keys which fail to unlock anything. Written in the margin of one papyrus we have, "When the wind comes, it veers toward the sycamore; / When you come . . ." And the rest is lost.

It is a long journey from the decaying fragments of stone and papyrus upon which ancient Egyptian literature is written to finished translations of that civilization's classics. Shown only the shattered pieces, one is bound to ask, with Ezekiel, can these bones live? Can these bits and pieces, these hints of old poems written three and four thousand years ago, poems and stories and wisdom from the time of Moses and before—from before even Abraham, predating his mythic wandering figure by centuries—can these fragments ever, through some miracle, come alive again to illuminate the thought and feeling—the consciousness—of their time, the days of their creators? Can they show us after so many centuries how men and women living in one of the first high civilizations—back at the very dawn of recorded history and conscience—thought, felt, and acted? Can they reveal to us how the human mind worked so long ago? Can not only the letter but also the spirit of the words be resurrected?

The answer, I think—admitting that the journey from stone to poem is dotted with pitfalls and that recovering Mind is much chancier than recovering stones and potsherds—the answer is largely "yes." We *can* "come upon the ancient people" (as Ezra Pound tried to do in his *Cantos* for over half a century: "to gather from the air a live tradition"); we *can* recover to a good degree the consciousness behind the shattered remnants of the words and literature of a great and enduring civilization. Though so often the texts, as we now have them, are fragmentary, many are, or can be made, almost or entirely complete; we *can* determine a hieroglyphic text upon which to base a translation; and we *do* know enough of the Egyptian language—its grammar, vocabulary, clause structure, and, for poetry especially, its style—to derive a believable English translation from the original.

How do we proceed? If a complete text is available, say, on a clean, untattered, neatly written papyrus, one then proceeds directly to transcribing the hieratic handwriting into hieroglyphs; and from there, one begins a literal translation of the text into English. But much Egyptian literature must be reconstructed; it must be slowly and painstakingly put together from small pieces. The process is analogous to completing a jigsaw puzzle—with the added complication that for the same final picture we have pieces from different copies, all cut differently and all in the same horrendous pile to be sorted out and made sense of. And usually we have too many pieces that fit in one part, overlapping and confusing each other, while there are all too often pieces missing from other parts.

If the scholar is fortunate enough to possess multiple copies of a text, then the quality of each copy must be ascertained and an "eclectic" text developed, a single final text composed of the best readings from all the individual copies. Only then is the piece ready for translation.

This stage too is often laborious. Here the scholar aims at what is called a "literal" translation, transforming the hieroglyphs into English on a more or less word-for-word basis. Opinions differ as to just how free such a translation should be; my own practice has usually been to keep to the word-for-word version, including most of the Egyptian word- and clause-order, so that the next scholar can determine the choices I have made in the transfers from one language to another. This literal translation is the most important single stage of the progress from broken stone to final poem. Unfortunately, at this stage there is also no poem. The literal translation has not, and should not pretend to have, any literary value. Lovers of literature and poetry in English would recoil in horror at the butchery done to the language in many such translations; a late colleague has characterized this idiom of scholarly literality as "King-James-ese."

With the literal translation, then, we have only a skeleton of meaning: the poems are still dry bones, with no flesh upon them and no breath of life breathed into them. The text is still the document of the philologist and not yet the living creature of the poet, not yet possessing, as is often said in literary studies, an independent life of its own—as the masterwork outlives its creator. How does one go that last stage of the journey? How to move from literal to literary? How to transmute a "text" into a "poem"?

In this final stage the translator must shift his or her value system from that of the scholar—cautious, meticulous, analytic, skeptical, scientific—to that of the poet—spontaneous, synthetic, imaginative, emotional, and whatever other qualities one may wish to attribute to the creative artist. The translator-poet, of course, begins with a text whose words and literal meaning must be respected, else new poems are created instead of poetic translations of meaning from another language.

And what interests the poet-translator in that literal text are the same facts and qualities we seek in reading modern poems. We want to know who is speaking the poem, who the characters are, where the situation takes place, and what happens. We also want to know the thoughts and feelings of the persons in the poem, their attitudes and emotions. And we look for words well-placed and things excellently said; that is, we also look for quality in the poet's use of tools, and we thus want excellence of workmanship and style. In a word, we want to be treated to a single, unified, compelling moment (or series of moments) of human experience. And for an Egyptian poem translated into English, that means an attempt to recover patches of human experience from three and four thousand years ago. The speakers of these poems must stand alive before us once again to show us why those now-anonymous Egyptian poets wanted to put their times and people into words. In this way, the life of an exile, Sinuhe, in the pharaonic Egypt of the twentieth century B.C. can be recovered to enrich the lives of those in the twenty-first century A.D.

So, as the translator-poet works on these texts, he or she looks for the incident or emotion or mood that seems to have inspired the original poem, from which it grew in the Egyptian poet's imagination. And the translator looks for images and turns of phrase and connotations attached to the literal words, listening, as Dylan Thomas once said, in order "to hear words whispering to one another." And it is from such elements, and from the recreative imagination, that the modern translator revivifies the poem: it becomes the *text transfigured*. And if the translator is lucky, talented, experienced in the original language, and has worked hard at the craft of words in English, then, perhaps, the result is a poem which can delight and even illumine the modern reader or hearer. The literal translation communicates only one kind of meaning, the "intellectual." But there are other kinds—emotional meaning; imaginative meaning; and the meaning conveyed by tone, images, metaphors, and symbols, all of which contribute to the "multidimensional" language of poetry. In the literary translation, these other kinds of meaning are included; more is attempted, and when successful, more is recovered from the dust-heaps of the past.

v

What is the rightful place of ancient Egyptian literature in world literature? Along with the Sumero-Akkadian literature, it is the world's first—the earliest expression of humankind's experiences and hopes and dreams; of the human encounter with nature and the gods, with other persons, with people of other nations—sometimes hostile—with daily life, with miracles, with the ups and downs of society and politics, and with our own inner, sometimes turbulent or bewildered, selves. It is, even now, a rich literature, despite the fact that it lies before us in ruins. Enough remains for us to insist flatly that its masterpieces belong at the beginning of our traditions of world literature— as the fountainhead—preceding the contributions of Greece and Israel. An entire era of our human venture—lasting approximately two millennia—produced sometimes brilliant literary pieces; and of this era we know very little. Fascinated as we are by pyramids and mummies, we know almost nothing of Egypt's verbal heritage. Yet that inheritance is ours also; and we have been too long blinded by our own formative traditions to appreciate the older, sometimes deeper, and now alien excellence of Egypt and the other high cultures of the ancient Near East.

Finally, all translators worth their salt want, with Pound, to "make it new" for their own times and languages. Yet, in closing, I also want to stress that these translations are meant to be a critical reading of the ancient Egyptian poetic texts in the original—a reading Egyptologists, too, I trust, can address with profit. The poems result from an affection for the culture, people, language, and poetry of ancient Egypt that is of many years' standing; and my intent is that these echoes of the ancient voices ring true.

ACKNOWLEDGMENTS

There are many persons to whom I owe thanks for kindnesses received over the years. First, to those who taught me the rudiments of Egyptology at the Oriental Institute of the University of Chicago: John Wilson, George Hughes, Charles Nims, Klaus Baer, and Edward Wente. I have also regularly profited from contact with colleagues and friends at the Institute: Janet Johnson, Peter Dorman, Lanny Bell, Robert Ritner, Mark Lehner, Ray Johnson, Karen Wilson, Emily Teeter, John Larson, Anita Ghaemi, Ray Tindell, Jean Grant, Chuck Jones, John Sanders, and Tom Urban.

Thanks, too, to the Oriental Institute for permission to use its copy of MacScribe to compose the hieroglyphic passages in this volume.

I also want to thank the members of The American Research Center in Egypt (ARCE) and the Society for the Study of Egyptian Antiquities for listening to and commenting on the papers I have offered over the years at the annual meetings of these societies. I have received much helpful criticism.

Thanks also to John Dorman, who was director of ARCE when I first went to Egypt and aided me in numberless ways, and to Mark Easton, until recently Cairo Director of ARCE, for many kindnesses over the years.

I am grateful for fellowships given me by the National Endowment for the Humanities as well as those from Roosevelt University, and for a grant from the American Philosophical Society. These awards fundamentally aided me in pursuing my study of ancient Egyptian literature.

Thanks are also due to Jim Burr, Humanities Editor, Leslie Tingle, Assistant Managing Editor, and their colleagues at the University of Texas Press for their interest in my work and for seeing this volume through the process of publication.

I am indebted more than I can adequately express to my family, who have borne with me for four decades, usually with good humor, in my double career as Professor of English and translator-scholar of Egyptian literature — to Ann, Kristen, and Robert, my children (historians all) — and to Gloria, my patient and always supportive wife.

Finally, my thanks to the many friends in the field in this hemisphere, Europe, and Egypt — nameless here but vivid in the mind — for their help, cautions, and succor over the years.

Ancient Egyptian Literature

Akhenaten's *Hymn to the Sun*, Stanza i

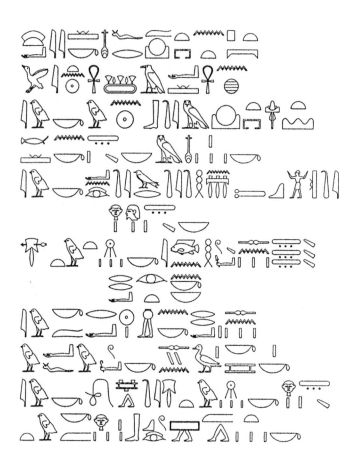

Akhenaten's *Hymn to the Sun*

COMPOSED CIRC. 1350 B.C., possibly by King Akhenaten himself (who is the speaker of the poem), this hymn exalts the one God who created heaven and earth—but here in His visible (not hidden) form as the Sun, which makes all life possible. The poet's loving emphasis upon nature and God's creatures and upon the beauty and variety of creation is obvious. Akhenaten is presented as the bodily Son of God and intercedes with Him for humankind.

Akhenaten's *Hymn to the Sun*

i

Let your holy Light shine from the height of heaven,
     O living Aton,
               source of all life!
From eastern horizon risen and streaming,
     you have flooded the world with your beauty.
You are majestic, awesome, bedazzling, exalted,
               overlord over all earth,
        yet your rays, they touch lightly, compass the lands
                    to the limits of all your creation.
There in the Sun, you reach to the farthest of those
     you would gather in for your Son,
               whom you love;
Though you are far, your light is wide upon earth;
     and you shine in the faces of all
               who turn to follow your journeying.

ii

When you sink to rest below western horizon
               earth lies in darkness like death,
Sleepers are still in bedchambers, heads veiled,
               eye cannot spy a companion;
All their goods could be stolen away,
               heads heavy there, and they never knowing!
Lions come out from the deeps of their caves,
               snakes bite and sting;
Darkness muffles, and earth is silent:
               he who created all things lies low in his tomb.

iii

Earth-dawning mounts the horizon,
>   glows in the sun-disk as day:
You drive away darkness, offer your arrows of shining,
>   and the Two Lands are lively with morningsong.
Sun's children awaken and stand,
>   for you, golden light, have upraised the sleepers;
Bathed are their bodies, who dress in clean linen,
>   their arms held high to praise your Return.
Across the face of the earth
>   they go to their crafts and professions.

iv

The herds are at peace in their pastures,
>   trees and the vegetation grow green;
Birds start from their nests,
>   wings wide spread to worship your Person;
Small beasts frisk and gambol, and all
>   who mount into flight or settle to rest
>   live, once you have shone upon them;
Ships float downstream or sail for the south,
>   each path lies open because of your rising;
Fish in the River leap in your sight,
>   and your rays strike deep in the Great Green Sea.

v

It is you create the new creature in Woman,
>   shape the life-giving drops into Man,
Foster the son in the womb of his mother,
>   soothe him, ending his tears;
Nurse through the long generations of women
>   to those given Air,
>   you ensure that your handiwork prosper.

When the new one descends from the womb
        to draw breath the day of his birth,
You open his mouth, you shape his nature,
        and you supply all his necessities.

vi

Hark to the chick in the egg,
        he who speaks in the shell!
    You give him air within
            to save and prosper him;
And you have allotted to him his set time
        before the shell shall be broken;
Then out from the egg he comes,
        from the egg to peep at his natal hour!
    And up on his own two feet goes he
        when at last he struts forth therefrom.

vii

How various is the world you have created,
        each thing mysterious, sacred to sight,
O sole God,
        beside whom is no other!
You fashioned earth to your heart's desire,
        while you were still alone,
Filled it with man and the family of creatures,
        each kind on the ground, those who go upon feet,
            he on high soaring on wings,
The far lands of Khor and Kush,
        and the rich Black Land of Egypt.

viii

And you place each one in his proper station,
        where you minister to his needs;

Each has his portion of food,
        and the years of life are reckoned him.
Tongues are divided by words,
        natures made diverse as well,
Even men's skins are different
        that you might distinguish the nations.

ix

You make Hapy, the Nile, stream through the underworld,
        and bring him, with whatever fullness you will,
To preserve and nourish the People
        in the same skilled way you fashion them.
You are Lord of each one,
        who wearies himself in their service,
Yet Lord of all earth, who shines for them all,
        Sun-disk of day, holy Light!
All of the far foreign countries —
        you are the cause they live,
For you have put a Nile in the sky
        that he might descend upon them in rain —
He makes waves on the very mountains
        like waves on the Great Green Sea
           to water their fields and their villages.

x

How splendidly ordered are they,
        your purposes for this world,
        O Lord of Eternity, Hapy in heaven!
Although you belong to the distant peoples,
        to the small, shy beasts
        who travel the deserts and uplands,
Yet Hapy, he comes from Below
        for the dear Land of Egypt as well.

And your Sunlight nurses each field and meadow:
>> when you shine, they live,
>>>> they grow sturdy and prosper through you.
You set seasons to let the world flower and flourish—
>> winter to rest and refresh it,
>>>> the hot blast of summer to ripen;
And you have made heaven far off
>> in order to shine down therefrom,
>>>> in order to watch over all your creation.

xi

You are the One God,
>> shining forth from your possible incarnations
>>>> as Aton, the Living Sun,
Revealed like a king in glory, risen in light,
>> now distant, now bending nearby.
You create the numberless things of this world
>>>> from yourself, who are One alone—
>> cities, towns, fields, the roadway, the River;
And each eye looks back and beholds you
>> to learn from the day's light perfection.
O God, you are in the Sun-disk of Day,
>> Over-Seer of all creation
>>>> —your legacy
>>> passed on to all who shall ever be;
For you fashioned their sight, who perceive your universe,
>> that they praise with one voice
>>>> all your labors.

xii

And you are in my heart;
>> there is no other who truly knows you
>>>> but for your son, Akhenaten.

May you make him wise with your inmost counsels,
                    wise with your power,
          that earth may aspire to your godhead,
                    its creatures fine as the day you made them.
Once you rose into shining, they lived;
          when you sink to rest, they shall die.
For it is you who are Time itself,
          the span of the world;
                    life is by means of you.

Eyes are filled with beauty
                    until you go to your rest;
All work is laid aside
                    as you sink down the western horizon.

Then, Shine reborn!   Rise splendidly!
          my Lord, let life thrive for the King
Who has kept pace with your every footstep
          since you first measured ground for the world.
Lift up the creatures of earth for your Son
          who came forth from your Body of Fire!

The Tale of the Shipwrecked Sailor

THE FOLLOWING story from the twentieth century B.C. is a tall tale or sailor's yarn—of shipwreck, a magic desert island, and a lordly talking snake. It is told in a seemingly simple and artless manner as befits a fairy tale. Yet the charm of the narration comes from the constant touches of humor, comedy, and irony that confirm that the author was a skilled composer of such narratives. The main story is framed by hints of another, just visible in the presence of the "leader" at its beginning and end. The sailor himself is a comic character—assertive, blustery, overconfident, forgetful of past favors, and unaware of the ironies of his speech and situation; and with the serpent's narration we actually have a tale within a tale within a tale.

The Tale of the Shipwrecked Sailor

The following was told by a master teller:

Be hale of heart, my leader!
        Look, we have come through!
The mallet has been taken, the mooring peg struck in,
        the forward rope secured upon the land;
Thanksgiving has been offered, God is praised,
        each man embraces his companion.
Your crew has come back safely,
        there are no losses to our expedition
Though we traversed the northern marches of Wawat
        and skirted Senmut Fortress.
Just look at us! we are successfully returned—
        this is our country; we are home!

Now, hear me out, my leader;
        I am a man who never stretches truth:
Purify yourself! pour water on your fingers!
        Thereafter you can answer what is put to you
That you address the King staunch-hearted,
        responding with no hesitation.
The mouth of a man can save him;
        speech can soften an angry face. . . .

        —Well, never mind.
You do whatever in the world you want, then;
        it gets to be a bother, talking to you!

But let me tell you just a little story, a bit like this,
        which happened once upon a time to me.
I was traveling to the region of the royal mines
        and had descended to the Great Green Sea

In a grand two-hundred-foot-long vessel
        (its width was seventy feet from rail to rail),
The crew within it, one hundred twenty
        of the finest men in Egypt:
Let them see only sky, let them see land,
        braver were their hearts than lions;
They could foretell a storm before its coming,
        foul weather before ever it occurred.

A storm came up—with us on the open sea—
        and no chance for us to reach harbor;
The wind grew sharp and made a constant moaning,
        and there were hungry fourteen-foot-high waves!
A piece of wood of some sort hit me,
        and then the ship was dead.
            Of all those fine men, not a one survived.

Then I was carried to a desert island
        by a swell of the Great Green Sea.
I spent three days alone,
        my heart my sole companion;
I nested in the shelter of a covering tree
        and hugged the shadows.
Finally, I stretched my legs
        in order to discover what to eat;
And I found figs and grapes there
        and every sort of tasty greens,
And sycamore figs, and notched figs,
        and cucumbers that looked cared for,
And fish, and birds—
        there was nothing that that island did not have!
Then I filled myself past satisfaction,
        spilling and dropping the abundance in my arms.
I shaped a fire drill, and made a fire,
        and gave burnt offering to the gods.

Then I heard a sound as of approaching storm,
            and I assumed it was another Great Green Sea wave—
                  trees were breaking, ground was quaking—
I bared my face
            and found it was a serpent coming my way:
The thing was over fifty huge feet long!
          its beard hung down a yard,
Its flesh was gilt,
           its eyebrows lapis lazuli;
               and it reared up in front.

It bared its mouth at me—
           I lying prone in fear and trembling—
              and spoke:
"What brings you? brings you?
           little man, what brings you?
If you delay to tell me
          what brings you to this isle,
I promise that you shortly shall be ashes—
           become like something that has never been."

"Though you just spoke to me,
          I am not all quite here to hear it;
I am, I know, before you
         but hardly know myself."

Then he put me in his mouth
          and took me to his place of residence
And set me down again without ill-treatment:
         I still was whole—no bites were out of me.
He bared his mouth once more—
         I on my belly on the ground before him—
           and said:

"What brings you? brings you?
             little man, what brings you
To this island of the Great Green Sea
             with shores as changing as the shifty waves?"

This time I told him all about it,
             my arms raised humbly in his presence,
                  saying:
"I was traveling to the region of the royal mines
             on an errand of the King
In a grand two-hundred-foot-long vessel
             (its width was seventy feet from rail to rail),
The crew within it, one hundred twenty
             of the finest men in Egypt:
Let them see only sky, let them see land,
             braver were their hearts than lions;
They could foretell a storm before its coming,
             foul weather before ever it occurred.
Each in his heart was steadier,
             his arm more powerful, than his companion —
                there was no sluggard in the lot!

"A storm came up — with us on the open sea —
             and no chance for us to reach harbor;
The wind grew sharp and made a constant moaning,
             and there were hungry fourteen-foot-high waves!
A piece of wood of some sort hit me,
             and then the ship was dead.
Of those fine men, not one survived, except for me —
             see, down here, beside you.
Then I was carried to this desert island
             by a swell of the Great Green Sea."

Then he said to me,
             "Fear not! fear not!

My little man, you must not pale your face so —
          you have reached me!
Look, God has let you live
          that he might bring you to this phantom isle.
There is nothing that it does not have,
          it is full of every fine and lovely thing!

"Now, you are going to spend one month, and then another,
          until you finish four months on this island.
Then a ship will come from Egypt
          with sailors in it whom you know
That you may go with them toward home
          and die in your own city.
What joy for one who lives to tell the things he has been through
          when the suffering is over!

"But let me tell you just a little story, a bit like yours,
          which happened on this very isle while I was here
               living with companions and my children
                    in one great extended family.
We totalled five and seventy persons,
          consisting of my offspring, relatives, and friends
(I cannot bear to dwell on a small daughter
          brought to me through prayer):

"A star fell
          and they were gone, gone up in flame.
It happened when I could not be there . . . all burned . . .
          and I not even with them.
I wanted to be dead instead of them
          after finding them a heap of tangled corpses.

"If you have courage, steel your heart
          that you may fill your arms with children,

And kiss your wife,
              and see your home.
Believe me, it is better than all else
              when you are back again
                    and dwell within the bosom of your friends."

Now I was lying stretched out on the ground,
              and I touched head to earth before him in respect:
"Let me say something to you:
              let me chronicle your glories for my King,
                    cause him to be acquainted with your highness;
Let me arrange to have them bring you precious ointments,
              balsam, spices, perfumes, sacred oils,
The finest temple incense
              that thrills the nostrils of each god;
Let me relate all that has happened to me
              as well as what I know at firsthand of your power
So they may properly praise God for your existence
              before the courts and councils of the Land;
Let me kill bulls to burn as offerings to you
              and wring the necks of birds;
Let me have them bring the fleet
              heaped with the fabled wealth of Egypt—
As one does for any god much loved by men
              who lives in a far country dimly known."

He laughed at me for what I told him—
              wrongly, to his way of thinking—
                    saying:
"Yours is no great supply of myrrh
              though it happens you have incense;
Why, I myself rule Punt,
              the myrrh from there is mine.
And that poor sacred oil you spoke of bringing—
              it is the main thing on this island!

Now, you in due time will remove from here
                    nevermore to see my island
                              which shall turn to trackless sea."

At last the ship arrived
                    just as he had foretold.
I climbed a lofty tree
                    and recognized the sailors in the ship
And went running to report it,
                    but he already knew.

Then he said to me,
                    "Fare well, fare well, my little man, off to your home
                              to see your children.
Make my name a proverb in your city;
                    my reputation rests with you."
I placed myself upon the ground,
                    my arms raised gratefully to him.

Then he collected me a cargo
                    of myrrh, the sacred oil, perfumes, spices,
Tishepes-spices, kohl, Punt perfume, giraffe tails,
                    great lumps of incense, elephant tusks,
Hounds, long- and short-tailed monkeys, and every helpful thing;
                    and I loaded all of it onto the ship.
I placed myself upon the ground again
                    giving praise to God for him.
Then he said to me,
                    "You shall reach your native land in two months time
To fill your arms with children
                    and grow young again at home until you die."
Then I descended to the shore near where the ship was.
                    I hailed the crew
And offered thanks beside the sea to the Lord of the Isle;
                    and those on board did likewise.

It was a voyage which we then made northwards
       toward the Royal City of the King;
And we arrived home after two months,
       just as he had said.
Then I entered to my Sovereign
       and presented him these gifts
          which I had fetched him from the island.
He offered thanks to God for my existence
       before the courts and councils of the Land;
And I was made a royal Follower
       and given two hundred servants.
Just look at me, once I touched land!
       and after seeing all that I had seen!

"Now, let what I have told sink in, my leader —
       you know, things people say can help you!"

Then he replied,
       "Don't try to play the expert, friend.
Does one give water to a sacrificial bird
       the morning of its execution day?"

Love Songs

LOVE SONGS are the most immediately appealing of all ancient Egyptian poems and need the least explanation. In them one finds the entire range of love situations and characters; and the tones and attitudes vary from chaste and idyllic to passionate and even erotic. Both males and females speak; and thus one sees both sides of love. These pieces all come from the Ramesside Period (ca. 1292–1070 B.C.) and derive from small collections or anthologies on papyri or ostraca now in London, or Turin, or Cairo. Love has hardly altered at all over the millennia.

"Why, just now, must you question your heart"

Why, just now, must you question your heart?
        Is it really the time for discussion?
To her, say I,
        take her tight in your arms!
For god's sake, sweet man,
        it's me coming at you,
My tunic
        loose at the shoulder!

"I love you through the daytimes"

I love you through the daytimes,
                        in the dark,
Through all the long divisions of the night,
                        those hours
I, spendthrift, waste away alone,
                        and lie, and turn, awake 'til whitened dawn.

And with the shape of you I people night,
                        and thoughts of hot desire grow live within me.
What magic was it in that voice of yours
                        to bring such singing vigor to my flesh,
To limbs which now lie listless on my bed without you?

Thus I beseech the darkness:
                        Where gone, O loving man?
Why gone from her whose love
                        can pace you, step by step, to your desire?

                        No loving voice replies.
And I (too well) perceive
                        how much I am alone.

"My love is one and only," lines 1–10

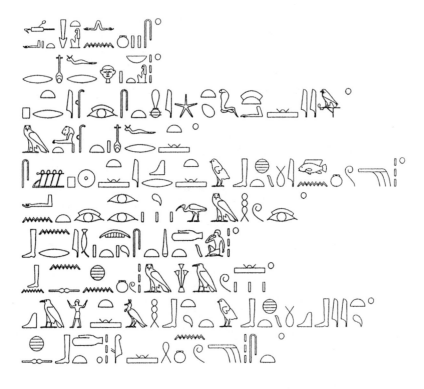

"My love is one and only"

My love is one and only, without peer,
        lovely above all Egypt's lovely girls.
On the horizon of my seeing,
        see her, rising,
Glistening goddess of the sunrise star
        bright in the forehead of a lucky year.
So there she stands, epitome
        of shining, shedding light,
Her eyebrows, gleaming darkly, marking
        eyes which dance and wander.
Sweet are those lips, which chatter
        (but never a word too much),
And the line of the long neck lovely, dropping
        (since song's notes slide that way)
To young breasts firm in the bouncing light
        which shimmers that blueshadowed sidefall of hair.
And slim are those arms, overtoned with gold,
        those fingers which touch like a brush of lotus.
And (ah) how the curve of her back slips gently
        by a whisper of waist to god's plenty below.
(Such thighs as hers pass knowledge
        of loveliness known in the old days.)
Dressed in the perfect flesh of woman
        (heart would run captive to such slim arms),
           she ladies it over the earth,
Schooling the neck of each schoolboy male
        to swing on a swivel to see her move.
(He who could hold that body tight
        would know at last
           perfection of delight —

Best of the bullyboys,
first among lovers.)
Look you, all men, at that golden going,
like Our Lady of Love,
without peer.

"Love, how I'd love to slip down to the pond"

Love, how I'd love to slip down to the pond,
                  bathe with you close by on the bank.
Just for you I'd wear my new Memphis swimsuit,
                    made of sheer linen, fit for a queen—
Come see how it looks in the water!

Couldn't I coax you to wade in with me?
                  Let the cool creep slowly around us?
Then I'd dive deep down
            and come up for you dripping,
Let you fill your eyes
            with the little red fish that I'd catch.

And I'd say, standing there tall in the shallows:
Look at my fish, love,
         how it lies in my hand,
How my fingers caress it,
           slip down its sides . . .

But then I'd say softer,
            eyes bright with your seeing:
                    A gift, love. No words.
            Come closer and
                look, it's all me.

"Love of you is mixed deep in my vitals"

Love of you is mixed deep in my vitals,
        like water stirred into flour for bread,
Like simples compound in a sweet-tasting drug,
        like pastry and honey mixed to perfection.

O, hurry to look at your love!
        Be like horses charging in battle,
Like a gardener up with the sun
        burning to watch his prize bud open.

High heaven causes a girl's lovelonging.
        It is like being too far from the light,
Far from the hearth of familiar arms.
        It is this being so tangled in you.

"I think I'll go home and lie very still"

I think I'll go home and lie very still,
      feigning terminal illness.
Then the neighbors will all troop over to stare,
      my love, perhaps, among them.
How she'll smile while the specialists
      snarl in their teeth! —

      she perfectly well knows what ails me.

Songs of the Birdcatcher's Daughter, I–VIII

HERE BEGIN songs to distract the heart. Imagine in this girl the charm of your own love, dear to your heart, as she comes to you from the meadow.

Songs of the Birdcatcher's Daughter

I

Lover, beloved, strongwinged love,
        my heart like a huntress follows your flight.
A girl's sleepy feelings, wakened by you—
        you've made a whole world for me!

Here I am, breathless, fresh from my snares,
        birdgear still in my hands,
Throwstick and net . . . (I am ready) . . .
        For love of god, come ahunting!

Why, every last singer from Punt's here in Egypt,
        flew down covered with myrrh to the ears!
The first one came, and he pounced on my baitworm
        (odor of spice hung thick on the breeze),
And his talons were sticky with sweetgum.

        My heart turns to you, begging,
Let's free him together, we two,
        out where I have you alone.
Let yourself go, hear the voice (how he cries!)
        of my hostage crestfallen with myrrh.

How good it would be, just you there with me,
        while I set my carefullest trap!
And what luck for a lover—outbound for the marsh
        with that special one waiting to love!

II

Voice of the wild goose crying,
        calling me, caught by my lure . . .

But your loving me slows my going,
        tangled, I cannot work free.
Love, let me go,
        nets of my own need untying!

And what am I going to tell Mother?
        Each day's end returning to her
Bent double under my catch . . .
        Haiee! no tripping the snarelines today!
Wild goose, I hear your call,
        I'm captive, taken by love of you!

III

The wild goose bursts into flight, then settles
        beating his wings in distraction,
Mischiefmaker tearing the meshes,
        scourge of the birdcote.
Birds, thick as lizards, mill about squawking,
        and all is confusion.

I do not flutter, though caught
        (singing bird) in invisible net.
Lonely, I lift up my call
        under the weight of my love:

This heart is counterpoise to your own.
        I shall never be far.
Balance my love with your caring.

IV

Whenever I leave you, I go out of breath
        (death must be lonely like I am),
I dream lying dreams of your love lost,
        and my heart stands still inside me.

I stare at my favorite datecakes —
                they would be salt to me now,
And pomegranate wine (once sweet to our lips)
                bitter, bitter as birdgall.

Touching noses with you, love, your kiss alone,
                and my stuttering heart speaks clear —
Breathe me more of your breath, let me live!
                Man meant for me,
God himself gave you as his holy gift,
                my love to outlast forever.

V

What heaven it would be
                if my heart's own wish came true,
To care for all you have and are,
                housemistress of the manor!

While your arm lies gentle on my breast
                (which twists, unquiet, out of love),
I send my stealthy wish to creep inside you
                (praying, Deliver him to me!).
My love, O marry! be, in the darkness of this night,
                my lord, husband to me,
Or yet another girl walks lonely to her tomb.

                For who else gives good health and life?
Delight me with the air of your lifegiving,
                be prodigal,
Capitulate, let in
                this wandering heart which seeks you.

VI

The voice of the swallow, flittering, calls to me:
        "Land's alight! Whither away?"
No, little bird, you cannot entice me,
        I follow you to the fields no more.

Like you in the dawn mist I rose,
        at sunrise discovered my lover abed
          (his voice is sweeter).
"Wake," I said, "or I fly with the swallow."
And my heart smiled back
        when he, smiling, said:
"You shall not fly
        nor shall I, bright bird.
          But hand in hand
We shall walk the Nileside pathways,
        under cool of branches, hidden
          (only the swallow watching)—
Wide-eyed girl,
        I shall be with you in all glad places."
Can you match the notes of that song, little swallow?
        I am first in his field of girls!
My heart, dear sister, sings in his hand—
        love never harmed a winged creature.

VII

Let me look through his wayside gate—
        I think it's my love there, coming for me!
Eyes on the ground but my ears listening hard,
        I tremble a little, waiting for him.
(I'll make an art out of loving my love,
        he'll be my only concern!)
For him heart stops at nothing!

Why, he's sending me only a messenger!
                the one with fast slinky feet
Trusted with bedroom secrets
             . . . (I never liked him) . . .
A mere servant tells me my love's been a lie!
            "He's found another."

Whose turn is it now
            making soft eyes up into his face . . . ?

                  . . . o my god, love,
What kind of man breaks the heart of a girl
            with such ever so strange goings on?

VIII

My heart remembers how I once loved you,
            as I sit with my hair half done,
And I'm out running, looking for you,
            searching for you with my hair down!

If I ever get back, I'll weave
            an intricate hairdo down to my toes.
Love, there's so much time now to finish . . .

The Instruction for Little Pepi on His Way to School
The Satire on the Trades

THIS CHARMING piece belongs to the genre of "schoolboy texts"—a series of didactic poems and treatises written for fledgling scribes. Their aim is to teach young boys the duties and perquisites of the scribal profession and to warn them to avoid all pursuits that would interfere with learning—not only learning the hieroglyphs but also the proper conduct for a public official. Here, a father is giving advice to a seemingly reluctant young son as the two journey to the Royal City where Pepi is to be enrolled for his studies. The particular interest of this piece is the series of vignettes showing the hard lot of the artisans and unskilled workers. These vivid portraits of misery and even despair are meant to warn little Pepi of the kind of life that awaits him if he does not pay attention to his studies.

The work is difficult since its text must literally be reconstructed—it exists primarily through dozens of fragmentary ostraca, most with a stanza or less of writing on them. But enough exist so that an eclectic text of moderate certainty can be recovered to produce this tribute to education. It seems to have been one of the most frequently copied texts in the scribal schools of New Kingdom Thebes.

The Instruction for Little Pepi on His Way to School
The Satire on the Trades

i

Beginning of the Instruction
    composed by a man from Silê,
Kheti, Duauf's son,
    for his son, whose name was Pepi.
Now, Kheti was traveling upstream to the Royal City
    to enroll Pepi in the school for scribes
Among the children of the nobles
    and those most eminent at the palace.

ii

And he said to Pepi:
    "I have seen defeated, abject men! —
You must give yourself whole-heartedly to learning,
    discover what will save you from the drudgery of underlings.
Nothing is so valuable as education;
    it is a bridge over troubled waters.
Just read the end of the *Book of Kemyt*
    where you will find these words:
'A scribe in any position whatsoever at the royal palace
    will never be needy there.'

iii

" — And unless he shares his wisdom with other persons,
    he can never leave this life contented.
I do not see a calling equal to it
    and agree with what this wise book says.

Let me urge you to love learning more than your mother;
    have its perfections enter your mind.
It is more distinguished than any other occupation —
    there is nothing like it upon earth!
Good fortune grows for the scribe even from childhood,
    and people shall respect him;
They shall commission him to handle their affairs —
    nor will he go about dressed merely in a loincloth.

iv

"I do not see carvers sent on missions
    or goldsmiths in places where the scribe is sent.
But I have seen the coppersmith at work
    at the entrance to his kiln —
His fingers are like crocodile claws,
    and he stinks more than the spawn of fish.

v

"Any sort of artisan who takes up tools —
    he is as weary as the hoeman
Whose fields are full of sticks and troubles for the axe;
    only darkness saves him.
He has worked his arms to dropping in his labors,
    and it is nightfall when he lights his fire out there.

vi

"The mason cutting with his chisel
    in all sorts of hard and costly stone —
After he finishes two cubic feet of work,
    his arms are dead and he himself is weary.
He sits there until suppertime,
    knees cramped and with an aching back.

vii

"The barber barbers far into evening
      to earn a bit to swallow, a covering for his shoulders,
Taking himself from street to street
      to hunt down any who are ripe for barbering.
He is strong of arm to fill his belly
      just like the honeybee at work.

viii

"The reedcutter goes down into the marshes
      to gather shafts for arrows.
He has worked his arms to dropping in his labors,
      bugs and ticks have bitten him to death,
Sickness has laid him low —
      he fares no better than the damned.

ix

"The potter with his earth and clay —
      he rises early with the servants;
Weeds and swine hinder his efforts
      until he manages to fire his pots.
His clothing is stiff with slime
      and his leather apron is in tatters;
The air which enters up his nose
      spews directly from his kiln.
He makes a pestle of his feet
      to stamp the clay down flat,
Hacking up the courtyards of the houses,
      unwelcome in public places.

x

"Let me tell you about the builder of walls—
    life for him is pitiful.
Should he be outdoors in a cutting wind,
    he must keep on working in his loincloth;
His apron is mere rags
    and the rest-house far behind him.
His arms are dead from wielding the chisel,
    and every measurement is wrong;
He eats his food with his fingers
    and washes once a day.

xi

"The carpenter is wretched as he grasps his plan—
    the finishing of a chamber,
        an area in a tomb of six by ten.
A month goes by—
    its woodwork is torn down, its matting strewn about,
        and all that was so carefully constructed has been ruined.
As for providing for his own house,
    he cannot even feed his children.

xii

"The gardener fetching with the carrying-pole—
    his shoulders are the shoulders of old age;
His limbs are swollen from the yoke
    and he is skin and bones.
He spends the morning watering the vegetables
    and evening with the herbs;
He has labored in the sun
    and afterwards his body aches.
His speech slips back to death and his good name—
    he is too old for any other occupation.

xiii

"The farmer, he complains incessantly,
　　his cry more raucous than the raven's;
His fingers go about their duties
　　through all the raging of the storm;
Wearied beyond reward down in the marshes,
　　he becomes a living wreck.
His storehouse is depleted by the lions,
　　worse ills from hippopotami are his;
His creatures there lack dwellings
　　so he must leave them unprotected.
He reaches home exhausted
　　and the taxman cuts him down.

xiv

"The mat-maker in his tiny cubicle —
　　he is more wretched than a woman;
With his knees pressed against his stomach
　　he can hardly breathe.
If he wastes the day not weaving,
　　he is beaten with the leather fifty blows;
He must offer food to the door-guard
　　just to let him see the sun.

xv

"The arrow-maker is already spent
　　as he goes into the desert uplands.
What he must pay for donkeys is more costly
　　than their toil will profit in return;
And costly too his pay to country people
　　to point him on his way.
When he reaches home at evening,
　　the walking has exhausted him.

xvi

"The porter who treks to foreign lands
    has assigned his meager assets to his children;
Fearful alike of lions and of nomads,
    he has his wits about him only in Egypt.
He comes back home all woebegone:
    the journey has done him in.
He dresses in a loin-cloth for his clothing,
    and contentment never comes.

xvii

"The stoker has foul fingers,
    and the stink of him smells like the dead;
His eyes burn from too much smoke,
    and he can never ward off sickness.
He spends the day cutting up old rags,
    yet his own clothes are an abomination.

xviii

"The sandal-maker too is wretched,
    forever carrying his pots of grease and oil;
His shop is filled with skins of animal dead—
    he literally chews on leather.

xix

"The washerman washing on the riverbank
    bows low in the presence of the crocodile god.
'Father, let me go down to the edge of the water!'
    clamor his son and daughter.
Oh, there is no profession satisfies like this,
    distinguished above any other calling!—

He kneads all sorts of excrement,
    with not a limb of him left clean;
He does the undergarments of a woman
    full of the stains of her menstruation;
Tears are his daylong at the hot washing bowls
    or as he heaves the pounding stone;
The tub of dirty water whispers, 'Come to me
    and let me overflow because of you!'

xx

"The fowler too is poorly off
    as he stalks the guardians of heaven.
If a flock of birds pass over him,
    he cries, 'Oh, for a net!'
God will not let them fall into his hand—
    He makes the trapper's schemes miscarry.

xxi

"Let me tell you also of the fisherman;
    he is worse off than any other occupation
As he pursues his work on the River
    mingling with the crocodiles.
If he over-estimates the total of his harvest,
    he is in despair;
He cannot say, 'The crocodiles did this!'
    —it was his own fear blinded him.
As he goes forth upon the waters of the torrent,
    he cries, 'This is the very wrath of God!'

ם ם ם

"There is no occupation without its overseers—
    except for the scribe: he *is* the overseer.

xxii

"Now, if you will learn writing,
    it will be better
Than any of these trades which I have set before you—
    the guardian protects the fledglings in his care;
And a servant does not dare to tell his master,
    'Watch what you say to me!'
What I have done on this journey to the Residence
    was done for love of you.
Your days in school will be precious to you—
    their benefit will last to the end of time!
And may I be here to help you understand;
    let love of learning ease your opposition.

xxiii

"Now, let me say a bit concerning eloquence
    so you can leave behind what you have learned—
For instance, standing in the forum of contention,
    let it be you who counters with good counsel.
If one stretches to retort against a hot-head,
    one never knows the thing which drew his warmth.
Be candid with your audience
    and answer without delay.

xxiv

"If you walk in attendance on great men,
    keep to the rear.
If you are visiting a master in his home,
    and if his arms beckon someone else ahead of you,
Sit, hand over mouth,
    and do not ask for favors when beside him.
Do what he tells you
    and beware unravelled speech.

XXV

"Be serious
  and act with dignity.
Do not broadcast words that should be secret—
  the close-mouthed man constructs a shield about him;
And speak no hasty words
  while sitting with a man who is belligerent.

xxvi

"If you leave the schoolhouse
  after the midday break has been announced—
While you wander street to street among the neighborhoods,
  avoid the places of ill fame.

xxvii

"If an official sends you with a message,
  report it as he said it;
Do not omit, and do not add to it—
  the one he sends must be trustworthy.
He never will promote the careless,
  for he puts down in writing all his dealings;
Nothing can be concealed from him
  at any time, in any place.

xxviii

"Do not speak falsely of your background
  —that is disgusting to a man of eminence;
If your future offers what is good,
  his arms will welcome the ready heart of yesterday.
Do not bait a wrangling man—
  that too is disgusting
    to anyone who has to hear it.
If three loaves of bread can please you,

and swallowing two jugs of beer,
    and never fill your belly—beware!
To be most satisfying in another's service,
    avoid unguarded speech.

xxix

"Now, it is good to study many things
    that you may learn the wisdom of great men.
Thus you can help to educate the children of the people
    while you walk according to the wise man's footsteps.
The scribe is seen as listening and obeying,
    and the listening develops into satisfaction.
Hold fast the words which hearken to these things
    as your own footsteps hurry,
And while you are on your journey
    you need never hide your heart.
Step out on the path of learning—
    the friends of Man are your company.

xxx

"I have set you on the way of God;
    but the good fortune of a scribe rests on his own two shoulders
        from the day that he is born.
Should he reach the halls of judgment,
    it is the Council that will act as mentor to him.
No scribe lacks sustenance
    from the goods within the palace—
And that nursery of the gods is the sunshine on the scribe
    who gives himself to the teachings of wise men.

"Praise God for your father and your mother
    who have placed you on the pathway of the ever-living.
And now these things are set before you,
    for you, your children, and your children's children."

The Instruction for Little Pepi, Stanza xxix.

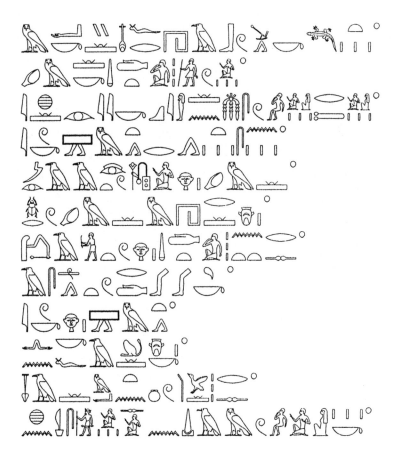

Longing for Memphis

THE SPEAKER of this poem is an apprentice scribe weary of his schoolwork and daydreaming of the big city. He prays to Ptah, god of Memphis, to help him concentrate on his lesson. The text is from a student's "miscellany" of New Kingdom date (ca. 1550–1070 B.C.).

Longing for Memphis

Farewell, my thoughts! Absconded,
      they race toward a place they know well,
Upriver bound to see Memphis, House of Lord Ptah.
      (And I wish I were with them!)

But I idle here absent-minded, wanting my thoughts back
      to whisper me news of the City.
No task at all now prospers by this hand—
      heart, torn from its perch, just not in it.

      (Come to me, Ptah! carry me captive to Memphis,
        let me gaze all around . . . and fly free!)

I would spend my workday wakeful and dutiful,
      but the will drowses, heart
Veers away, will not stay in my body;
      all other parts of me sickened to ennui—
The eye heavy with staring and studying,
      ear, it will not be filled with good counsel,
Voice cracks, and words of the recitation
        tumble and slur.

O Lord of the City friendly to young scribes,
      be at peace with me!
        Grant me to rise above this day's infirmities!

"Oh, I'm bound downstream on the Memphis Ferry"

T HE FOLLOWING piece shows the young scribe off to
the big city of Memphis, his duties at the scribal school
left behind him for a time. As he watches the Nile flow by, he senses the invisible presence of the gods. What began as a longing for a girl at Memphis
deepens into a love for the city and the gods who rule it.

"Oh, I'm bound downstream on the Memphis Ferry"

Oh, I'm bound downstream on the Memphis ferry,
        like a runaway, snapping all ties,
With my bundle of old clothes over my shoulder.

I'm going down there where the living is,
        going down there to that big city,
And there I'll tell Ptah (Lord who loves justice):
        "Give me a girl tonight!"

Look at the River! eddying,
        in love with the young vegetation.
Ptah himself is the life of those reedshoots,
        Lady Sakhmet of the lilies—
Yes, Our Lady of Dew dwells among lilypads—
        and their son, Nefertem, sweet boy,
Blossoms newborn in the blue lotus.
        Twilight is heavy with gods. . . .

And the quiet joy of tomorrow,
        dawn whitening over her loveliness:
O, Memphis, my city, beauty forever!—
        you are a bowl of love's own berries,
Dish set for Ptah your god,
        god of the handsome face.

Rebuke Addressed to a Dissipated Scribe

H ERE WE have a letter to a student who did not turn out well, written by a former teacher. Instead of attending to his studies the young scribe turns to a life of pleasure—drink and women. The teacher is obviously very disappointed.

Rebuke Addressed to a Dissipated Scribe

Now, as for what I have been told—
    that you throw aside your studies
        and live in a whirl of singing and dancing:

You go about from street to street,
    and beer fumes hang wherever you have been.
Don't you know beer kills the man in you?
    It stiffens your very soul!

You are like a warped steering-oar
    that gives no help to either side!
You are a shrine without its god,
    a house with no provisions!

You are discovered scrambling up a wall
    after breaking your confinement,
With people running headlong from you—
    you deal them bloody wounds!

If you only knew that strong drink is destruction,
    you would swear off the pomegranate wine,
You would not waste a thought on drinking-mugs,
    and you would disown beer!

You were taught to sing to the pipe,
    to perform to the reed-flute,
Chant in time to the lyre,
    and accompany the lute.

But you loll about the fancy houses,
    and the street girls swarm around you;

Or you stand there carrying on
  while they do their attendance on you.

You sit there under the hussy's spell,
  soaked with perfumes and ointments,
    with your wreaths of forget-me-nots round your neck;
Or you beat time on your gut as you stagger about,
  then fall down flat on your face
    and just lie there covered with filth.

Menna's Lament

Or Letter to a Wayward Son

THIS POEM appears on a magnificent ostracon in the Oriental Institute Museum at the University of Chi-cago. Menna, the father, and his son, Pay-iry, are historical personages of Ra-messide times (ca. 1292–1070 B.C.) who lived in the village of Deir el-Medineh on the west bank of ancient Thebes. The village supplied the workers who constructed and decorated the rock-cut tombs of the New Kingdom pharaohs in the Valley of the Kings. The ostracon derives ultimately from that village and its school for young scribes; and the letter is a literary rendering of a sad event that may actually have taken place. Pay-iry, instead of remaining at home and taking up his father's craft, runs off to sea. The bereft father writes in an attempt to persuade him to return.

Menna's Lament

Or Letter to a Wayward Son

The artist Menna
speaks to his son and apprentice,
the scribe, Pay-iry:

High winds foretell for you the coming of the storm,
        my able seaman, lost for the final mooring.

I had set good advice of every sort
        before you—but you never listened.
I would point out each path
        which hid the danger in the underbrush,
Saying, "Should you go without your sandals,
        one little thorn will end your caravan."
I satisfied your needs in everything
        which normal men desire;
Nor would I let you cry "If only!" in the night,
        tossing and turning as you lay in bed.

Yet you are like the swallow in her flight
        wide wandering with her fledgling brood;
And when you reach the Delta in your great migration,
        you run with foreign Asiatic birds—
You have fed on your own vitals
        and neither heart nor sense is left within you!

I am so troubled I would range the sea
        might I report that I had rescued you;
Yet would you come to enter your own village
        bringing but water for your monument.

I said in my heart, "He does not care for words,
            for any I have spoken up 'til now."

But I must say again what I have said before:

Get you from the ramparts of the wicked.
            Fortify yourself with maxims of the wise,
In speech, in name, in deed;
            and your ship of fools may still do likewise.
Then, should it founder far out in the East,
            men would address you with the honor due a lion
                        although you stood alone.

As for the son who should obey his father,
            that text holds good for all eternity, they say.
But then you did not pause for any admonition
            with which I warned and warned you long ago.

Should you capsize when you take ship defying me —
            should you drift downward to a watery grave —
Should you stride wide upon the waves to flee the deep —
            still were you lost through your own piloting!

And who shall speak the word to my small boat,
            "Go to him swiftly over the white-capped waves"?
I see you sinking in the chambers of the sea,
            and my arm does not know how to save you!
All I can bring you is a slender straw
            thrown in the wide path of the drowning man. . . .
                        There is not any way at all.

You make yourself like one who says
            that he would kill to have my donkeys,
                        choking the very protests in my mouth!

You clip the wings of one who eyes your goods,
        yet are you dull and dawdling in my presence;
Your goods themselves aggrandize only senseless people
        because you chose to act without me.

You should take care to weigh my words,
        and you might find my teaching useful;
Give ear to hear instruction
        so as to build on long experience.
Should I allow you to ignore it altogether,
        you will shoot up a useless weed;
There is no climbing to the height for such a one
        though he provide you with an ample household.

Oh, that a son of mine should be found out
        letting this hell-bent course continue!
You are like someone on a team of bolting horses,
        yet should your heart beat easy in the reins with mine!

My son, preserve and hold in trust this letter.
        Someday, it might bring you good.

The Debate between a Man Tired of Life and His Soul

THE FOLLOWING poem is a discussion—at times acrimonious—between a man so disspirited he wants to die and his *ba,* or soul, which insists that one must endure life until the end comes naturally.

The single surviving papyrus, its beginning lost, dates to Dynasty XII (ca. 1976–1793 B.C.). It is a profound text and difficult to translate. Yet the man's despair gives rise to some of the finest lyric poetry to survive from ancient Egypt.

The Debate between a Man Tired of Life and His Soul

i

.   .   .   .

[The man's ba-bird, or soul, is concluding a speech:]

.   .   .   .

"The tongues of the gods, they do not speak amiss,
       they make no special cases."

ii

I opened my mouth to my soul
       that I might answer what it had said:

"This is more than I can bear just now!
       —my soul could find no time for me!
It is beyond belief
       —as if I should hesitate to do the deed!
Let my soul not disappear like this, not flutter off,
       but let it take its stand beside me! —
Or never shall it have the chance
       to wrap my person in its stifling bonds;
And for all its twitter, never
       shall it escape the Day of Reckoning.

"O all you gods,
       see how my soul defames me!
I will not listen to it ever
       as I drag my way toward dissolution;
For it will not help me do the death by fire —
       myself the victim, who shall no more suffer.

"Let it be near me on the Day of Reckoning!
            Let it stand tall on that side yonder
                        as one who shares my joy!
Yet this the very soul that rushes off, it vanishes,
            to separate itself from death.
My foolish soul is going to ease the pains of living, is it?
            Keep me from death until I come to it by nature?

"No! make the West sweet for me now!
            Is there not pain and suffering enough?
—That is the stuff of life: a troubled journey, a circuit of the sun;
            even the trees decay and fall.

"O tread you down upon injustice,
            end my helplessness!
Judge me, O Thoth, you who can soothe the gods;
            defend, O Khonsu, me, a teller of the truth;
Hear, O Rê, my speaking, you who command the skyship;
            defend me, O Anubis, in the holy hall of judgment—
Because my need is heavy in the scale,
            and it has raised the pan of sweetness out of reach.
                        Preserve, O gods, the quiet center of my being!"

iii

What my soul said to me:

"You are no man at all!
            Are you even alive?
How full you are of your complaints of life
            like a man of means preaching to passersby!
Things sink down to ruin. Well! save yourself by getting up!
            There are no bonds on you as of some prisoner whining,
'I shall get even with you:
            and you, your name shall die!'

Life! That is the place of fluttering down,
        heart's own desire, the district of the West
           . . . after a troubled crossing."

iv

[*I continued:*]

"If my soul, my foolish brother, would only listen,
        its wish would be like mine;
And it would perch most blest at my right hand,
        reaching the West like one who has a pyramid
           towering for after-generations over his grave.

"And I would wave the sacred fan above your listless form
        that you attract another soul to join you, weary one;
And I would wave the fan again, then say the spell,
        so you might lure a different, fiery soul;
I would find drink from in-shore eddies, raise up food,
        beguile some other hungry soul to stay with you.
But if you keep me back from death this way,
        I promise you no peace in the West forever!

"Be still, my soul, my brother,
        until a successor comes with offerings
To stand at the tomb on burial day
        and deck a bed in the city of God."

v

Then my soul opened its mouth to me
        that it might answer what I had said:

"Your graveyard thoughts bring sadness to the heart,
        and tears, feeding our misery;
That is what shovels a man into his house
        dug in the rock on the high hill:

—There, there is no more coming forth for you
        to see the sunny days,
Or workmen crafting their buildings in granite,
        putting last touches on pyramids,
Or the beauties of the monuments,
        or where builders fashion altars for the gods:
—You are emptied and drear, like those without motion
        dead on the riverbank, no one caring:
Water laps at their backs,
        the sun does its work,
           and, lips in the current, fish whisper to them.

"Now listen to me—
        pay some attention to what people say:
           Spend your days happily! Forget your troubles!

"There was a man, and he farmed his plot of land;
        and he was loading his harvest into a ship
           for the voyage to his accounting, which drew near.
And he saw coming a night of wind and weather
        so that he was watchful of the ship, waiting for day,
While he dreamed of life with his wife and children
        who had perished on the Lake of Death
           on a dark night, with crocodiles.
And after he was pondering there some time,
        he shaped the silence into words, saying,
'I have not wept for that mother yonder—
        for her there is no returning from the West,
           no more than any who have lived on earth.
But let me mourn the children, killed in her womb,
        who saw the face of Death ere ever they were born.'

"There was another man, and he wanted his evening meat;
        and there was his wife, who said,
           'There will be bread.'

And he went outdoors to fume awhile
        and then go back inside
Behaving like a better person
        (his wife was wise to his ways).
Yet he never really listened to her,
        so the death demons came and carried him off."

vi

I opened my mouth to my soul
        that I might answer what it had said:

a

"How my name stinks because of you
        more than the stink of bird dung on a summer's day
            under a burning sky.
How my name stinks because of you
        more than the catch of fish on a good angling day
            under a burning sky.
How my name stinks because of you
        more than the stench of marsh-birds on the hummocks
            filthy with waterfowl.
How my name stinks because of you
        more than the fishermen's smell at runnels of swamps
            after they have been fishing.
How my name stinks because of you
        more than the reek of crocodiles sunning on sandbanks
            alive with their crocodile kind.
How my name stinks because of you
        more than the wife about whom lies
            are told to her wedded husband.
How my name stinks because of you
        more than the able youth of whom they falsely say
            that he is prisoner of everything he should despise.
How my name stinks because of you

more than the crocodile's cove, where the fool taunts him
careful his back is turned.

b

"Who is there to talk to today?
      Brothers are evil;
           the friends of today, they do not love us.
Who is there to talk to today?
      Hearts are rapacious;
           each man covets his neighbor's goods.
Who is there to talk to today?
      Gentleness is dead;
           brute strength bears down on everyone.
Who is there to talk to today?
      Men are proud of the evil they do;
           good everywhere falls defeated.
Who is there to talk to today?
      A man is maddened by evil fortune;
           the sad injustice moves all to laughter.
Who is there to talk to today?
      Robbery, plundering;
           each man a predator on his companion.
Who is there to talk to today?
      The malefactor masks as best friend;
           the trusted brother turns into an enemy.
Who is there to talk to today?
      There is no thought for tradition;
           no one nurturing decency these days.
Who is there to talk to today?
      Brothers betray;
           they take to strangers, not men of integrity.
Who is there to talk to today?
      Faces are wiped out;
           each, high or low, fighting all others.

Who is there to talk to today?
> Hearts are selfish and slick;
>> no heart to lean on.
Who is there to talk to today?
> There are no righteous men;
>> earth is abandoned to evil.
Who is there to talk to today?
> Emptiness in trusted friends;
>> blind ignorance to life that brings wisdom.
Who is there to talk to today?
> No man of satisfied mind;
>> one to walk quietly with does not exist.
Who is there to talk to today?
> I am bowed too low with my misery
>> lacking someone to share the thoughts in my heart.
Who is there to talk to today?
> Wrongdoing beats on the earth,
>> and of it there is no end.

c

"So death is before me now—
> the healthy state of sick man—
>> like coming out in the air after suffering.
So death is before me now
> like the fragrance of myrrh
>> or sailing at ease on a breezy day.
So death is before me now
> like aroma of flowers,
>> like being drunk in a promised land.
So death is before me now
> like the breath of a new Inundation,
>> like coming home from a long expedition.
So death is before me now
> like a clearing sky,
>> like understanding what perplexed us before.

So death is before me now
    like one longing to see his home
        after long years in prison.

    d

"But to be one who is over there
    with living God
        fighting evil for Him who made him!
But to be one who is over there
    erect in the skyship
        offering choice gifts to the temples!
But to be one who is over there!
    One who finally, perfectly knows!
        And he shall never be kept from approaching great God
            whenever he would speak!"

vii

What my soul said to me:

        "Put your murmuring aside now.

"O you who belong to me, my brother,
        must you be sacrifice upon the flaming altar?
Friend, fight on the side of life!
        Say to me, 'Love me *here!*'
Put thoughts of the West behind you!
        Love! yes, love, indeed,
So that you may in due time reach the West,
        may touch your body gently to the earth;
And I shall flutter down beside you
        when you are weary of the world at last.
            Then shall we two be fellow citizens together."

The Resurrection of King Unis

THIS VERY ancient hymn—from about 2320 B.C., toward the beginning of surviving Egyptian literature—can still be seen carved on the wall of the burial chamber of King Unis of Dynasty V in the Old Kingdom. It commemorates the death of the king—or, better, his transfiguration from inert body to active power in his true home among the gods. The author envisions a communion feast in which lesser gods are hunted down, butchered and boiled, and then eaten by King Unis so as to neutralize their power and so that their essence will revive and nourish him and enhance his power. There is no evidence for cannibalism during historic times in Egypt; and such a religious ceremony indicates very ancient roots for the poem.

The Resurrection of King Unis

i

A pale sky darkens,
        stars hide away,
Nations of heavenly bowmen are shaken,
        bones of the earth gods tremble—
All cease motion, are still,
        for they have looked upon UNIS, the King,
Whose Soul rises in glory, transfigured, a god,
        alive among his fathers of old time,
            nourished by ancient mothers.

ii

The King, this is he! Lord of the twisty ways of wisdom
        (whose very mother knew not his name),
His magnificence lights the black sky,
        his power flames in the Land of the Risen—
Like Atum his Father, who bore him;
        and once having born him,
            strong was the Son more than the Father!

The *Kas* of the King hover about him;
        feminine spirits steady his feet;
Familiar gods hang over him;
        uraei rear from his brow;
And his guiding Serpent precedes:
        "Watch over the Soul!
            Be helpful, O Fiery One!"
All the Mighty Companions are guarding the King!

iii

The King, this is he! strong Bull of the Sky
         with blood-lust in his heart,
Who feasts on the incarnation of each god,
         eating the organs of those
Who come, their bodies fat with magical power,
         fresh from the Isle of Flame.

iv

The King, this is he! his Change now accomplished,
         united again with his blessed Spirits.
The King is arisen, transfigured, become this great God,
         lord over acolyte gods;
He sits
         and his back is toward earth.

v

The King, this is he! who deals out judgment
         sitting in concert with One
            (whose Name must ever be hidden)
         this day when sacrifice comes to the first-born.

The King, this is he! lord of the offering meal,
         he knots the sacred cord,
            provides his own gifts for the altar.

The King, this is he! who eats men,
         feeds upon gods;
Keeper of tribute victims,
         he renders swift sentence.

vi

It is Seizer of Scalp-locks who ropes them in for the King;
        He of the Upreared Head it is hobbles them,
            dragging them near for him;
The Chief over Blood Rites binds them,
        and Traveler throws down the Lords-god
That he might cut their throats for the King,
        cut from their bodies what is inside them —
This is the envoy of judgment he sends
        to deal execution.
And then the Bloody-eyed butchers them,
        cooks the pieces of them for the King,
            filling his kettles at dinnertime.

vii

The King, this is he! who eats down their magic,
        swallows their vital power.
Their biggest belong to his meal at daybreak;
        those in between are for dinner;
Their smallest are his provisions at nightfall;
        and their old men and women?
            —sticks for his hearth-stones!

Great gods of the northern heaven lay fire to his stew-pots —
        their contents the thighs of the first-born.
Sky-dwellers fly about serving the King,
        stirring his kettles with legs of their women.
They travel throughout the Twin Heavens for him,
        they people the world's Two Shores.

viii

The King, this is he! a great Power,
        potent among the all-Powerful!

The King, this is he! hawk-image of the divine,
    best likeness among fierce forms of the Great One
      —hungriest of the hunters:
Any he finds in his way,
    he eats him down bit by bit.
Oh, the King's proper seat is surely as Chief,
    before the ranked Great in the Land of Glory!

The King, this is he! a god,
    older than eldest;
Thousands go about serving him,
    hundreds there are heap his offering tables.

There has been given him certification and warrant:
    "This one is one of the Great Gods!"
      thus says Orion, ancestral father.

ix

The King has risen again, translated to heaven;
    and the Bodily Form shines forth,
      Lord of the Land of the Glorified!
He has shattered the bones of the vertebrae,
    seized on the hearts of the gods;
He has dined upon blood,
    swallowed down the fresh pieces,
To be nourished by lungs of the wise ones,
    to be warmed with life from their hearts
      and their magic power as well.
Upraised is the King (look, he rises!)
    to feast on the bits afloat in the red broth!
And the Bodily Form, it stirs! it quickens!
    their magic is working within him!
Nevermore can his heavenly glory be gone from him:

he has taken unto himself
the genius of every god.

x

The time of the King now, it is eternity,
his boundaries, they touch infinity,
Through this his power to do what he will,
avoid whatever he hates,
concerning all things in the kingdom of heaven
throughout all space and time.

xi

So now, their souls are at home within the King's body,
their turbulent energy under his spell,
Through this his communion consisting of gods,
boiled for the King from their bones.

So now, their souls are the King's subjects,
and the ghosts are gone from their broken forms.
The King is free from all these!
Risen! Arisen!
Lasting! Everlasting!
NEVERMORE shall the power of deities be deadly
who would hack the abode where the heart of UNIS
dwells 'mid the living on this our earth
for ever and ever more.

The Transfiguration of the King

Hymns and Prayers from the Pyramid Texts

T HE PYRAMID Texts are the world's earliest substantial body of religious writings. They were carved and painted in the pyramid chambers of the last king (Unis) of Dynasty V and several of the kings of Dynasty VI (ca. 2322–2191 B.C.). They comprise magical spells, exhortations, hymns, and prayers—all meant to aid the deceased pharaoh (who was after all a god king) in returning to his proper sphere with the gods. As one reads the next several poems, one is impressed by the tremendous upward thrust conveyed by the imagery; for in this early stage of ancient Egyptian religion, particularly as regards the king, the location of the Afterworld (or the "Horizon") is felt to be somewhere in the sky. Once his upward journey is completed, aided by the cosmic gods, the king will take his place for eternity in a renewed life with his peers.

Prayer to the King to Rise Up
Pyramid Text 373

Oho!   Oho!
    Raise yourself up, O King Teti!
Take back your head,
    gather your bones;
Collect your limbs,
    shake the earth from your flesh;
Receive your food which does not stale,
    your drink which does not sour.

You shall stand at the gates which bar mere mortals,
    and Khentymenutef shall come to you
To grasp your hand
    and take you to the sky to Geb, your father.

And Geb will rejoice in your coming;
    and he will stretch out his arms to you,
And kiss you,
    and hold you.
And he will place you first among transfigured spirits
    and inextinguishable stars,
        and those from hidden seats will praise you.

The Great appear that they may serve you,
    the guardian gods stand guard;
Barley is threshed
    and emmer reaped for you,
Served at your monthly festivals,
    served at your mid-month feast days—
All this as ordered by your father Geb.
    Rise up, King Teti!   You have not died!

Hymn to the King as a Primordial God
Pyramid Text 486

Hail, primeval waters, which Shu brought forth and the twin springs raised,
    where Geb purified his body,
While hearts were pervaded by fear
    and minds were numb with terror!

I, King Pepi, was born in that Chaos
    before there was sky, before there was earth,
Before there were heavenly pillars, or strife,
    or the fear that came through the Eye of Horus.

I, King Pepi, am one of that body of Great Ones
    born long ago in Heliopolis,
Who are not carried off because of a king,
    not taken away before magistrates,
Not punished with death,
    not found guilty.

Such am I, King Pepi!
    I shall not be punished with death,
Not carried off because of a king,
    not taken away before magistrates.
My enemies shall not be victorious,
    I shall not be poor;
My nails shall not grow long
    nor the bones in me be broken.

Should I go down to the primal Chaos,
    Osiris will raise me up, the Two Conclaves of gods will shoulder me,
And Rê will give me his hand to take me
    wherever a god may dwell.

And should I go down into earth,
  Geb will raise me up, the Two Conclaves of gods will shoulder me,
And Rê will give me his hand to take me
  wherever a god may dwell.

Hymn to the King as a Flash of Lightning
Pyramid Text 261

This is the King, who startles the heart, darling of air,
    far-stretched across the sky, a blinding light.
This is the King, a flame before the wind,
    to the limits of heaven, the ends of earth,
        until his blazing bolt is gone.
The King treads the air, strides over earth,
    kisses the waters of the ur-god's high hill.
Those at the zenith open their arms to him;
    and he stands on the heights of the eastern sky.
He has reached the end of his journey!
    This is the King, the messenger of storm.

Prayer of the King as a Star Fading in the Dawn
Pyramid Text 216

I have come to you, O Nephthys;
    I have come to you, Sun Barque of Night;
I have come to you, You Who are Just in the Reddening;
    I have come to you, Stars of the Northern Sky—
        remember me.

Gone is Orion, caught by the underworld,
    yet cleansed and alive in the Beyond;
Gone is Sothis, caught by the underworld,
    yet cleansed and alive in the Beyond.
Gone am I, caught by the underworld,
    yet cleansed and alive in the Beyond.

It is well with me, with them,
    it is quiet for me, for them,
Within the arms of my father,
    within the arms of Atum.

The Prophecy of Neferty

T HE FOLLOWING is a vision or prophecy written most probably during the reign of King Amenemhat I (ca. 1976–1947 B.C.), the founder of Dynasty XII. However, it is set back during the reign of King Sneferu (ca. 2614–2579 B.C.), founder of the Fourth Dynasty of the Old Kingdom. Sneferu requires some entertainment; and the seer Neferty from Heliopolis is recommended to him because of his wisdom and his ability to see into the future. He prophesies a time of turmoil ahead when Egypt will be overrun by foreigners from the East. They will conquer the northeast Delta, bringing death and devastation. It is as if the world had slid back into the original chaos so that Rê must begin creation over again. But a savior will come from the Southland (Amenemhat I) who will defeat the enemy and bring order back to Egypt. The poem is obviously a piece of propaganda extolling the rule of Amenemhat I; but the words of Neferty are often fine poetry.

The Prophecy of Neferty

It all occurred back when the Majesty of Egypt, Sneferu,
      was mighty King throughout the land.
         And one fine day this happened:

The Royal Council made an entrance
      into the palace to offer their respect,
Moving in ordered procession to report on their concerns
      as was their daily custom.

Then said his Majesty to the messenger beside him,
      "Go. Bring the Royal Council to me
Which has come to pay obeisance on this day."
      And those he brought were ushered in immediately.

Then they were upon their stomachs, prone
      in the presence of his Majesty once more;
And he said to them, "Comrades,
      I have had you summoned
         so that you might search out for me
A son of yours with wisdom, a brother of yours with skill,
      or a friend of yours to furnish entertainment,
Who shall offer me a bit of eloquence
      or some choice wisdom which my Majesty delights to hear."

They placed themselves upon their stomachs, prone
      in the presence of his Majesty once more,
Saying,
      "There is a lector priest, a high priest of Bastet,
         O Sovereign our Lord, whose name is Neferty.
He is a commoner, of valiant arm,
      a scribe quick with his fingers,

And a wealthy man, richer than all his peers.
    If only he be fetched, his Majesty might see!"

Then said his Majesty, "Go, bring him to me!"
    And he was brought to him forthwith.
He stretched out upon his stomach, prone
    in the presence of his Majesty,
Who said,
    "Pray come, Neferty, my friend,
So that you might offer me a bit of eloquence
    or some choice wisdom which my Majesty delights to hear."

The lector Neferty then said,
    "About what has already happened
        or of things that are to be, O Sovereign my Lord?"
His Majesty, "Of things that are to be.
    Today is here already. Let it pass."

Then he reached for a box of writing tools
    and took a clean papyrus and a palette,
And he himself put into writing
    what was said by the lector Neferty.

Now Neferty was a wise man of the East,
    one who served Bastet at her theophanies;
His origins were in the nome of Heliopolis,
    and he cared for what would happen to the land.
And he foresaw the conquest from the East
    when Asiatics went about in all their power,
When they terrorized the hearts of those who were at harvest,
    when they carried off the ox-teams meant for plowing.

And so he said,

"Be stirred, my heart,
    that you may mourn this land whence you have sprung!
Yet weep not overmuch—
    for what I say is god's own truth:

"See how the eminent are mocked and thrown upon the ground
    in the land whence you have sprung!
Do not hold back! Set it before your eyes
    that you may stand against what rises in your presence!

"—There shall be no more nobles to act as counsel for the land;
    all that has been achieved no better than the primal chaos,
        so that Rê must start creation over again!
The land is perished utterly, no saving remnant left,
    no need to hold one second from its doom!

"Our land is hurt, and there are none who care,
    none who speak out, none offer tears!
The land shall be as if the Sun were shrouded,
    his brilliance lacking, by which men might see;
One cannot live when storm clouds lower—
    all are darkened when bereft of Him.

      "—I must speak out what is before my sight;
        I do not prophesy what shall not be:

"Egypt's River shall run dry
    so that one may walk dry-shod across it;
They shall seek water for the ships to sail on—
    the River's course is now but dusty land.
Riverbank shall turn to flood,
    and water's home shall be the place for shore.
Southwind shall dispute with Northwind
    and no sky have an unmixed breeze.

"A strange bird shall be engendered
        in the marshes of the Northland:
He has built a nest beside the citizens
        so that our people bear him of necessity.
Perished away those spots of beauty:
        the lakes and curving pools, gleaming, full of game-birds,
Fountains with familiar fish and fowl—
        oh, all things bright and beautiful are gone!
The land lies stretched in pain
        because of those robber-birds, those birds of prey,
                those Asiatics who defile the land.

"Enemies shall come upon us from the East—
        Asiatics have descended into Egypt!
The border fort is stormed, the next one on—
        nevermore their garrisons be heard from!
They shall climb the ladders in the night,
        enter the fortresses and council chambers!

                "—And they shall banish slumber from my eyes
                        whether I would be sleeping or awake!

"Wild desert beasts shall come to drink the water
        down by Egypt's River;
So shall they be at ease upon the riverbanks made theirs
        for lack of those to tame them.
This land is seized by savages, who come untaught,
        and the fruits of what shall happen hide from speech:
Seeing and hearing shall be blurred and deafened,
        and silence is in sight. . . .

                "—Let me offer you a land like sickness
                        where what should not happen does:

From *The Prophecy of Neferty*

"They shall take weapons of war
    so that the land is alive with tumult.
They shall make arrows of copper,
    bread shall be paid for in blood.
Let them laugh with the laughter of pain,
    no tears shall be spared for the dead;
One cannot assuage the wants of the dying—
    the heart of a man first looks to himself.

"There are none who show sorrow these days,
    and the heart is wholly bewildered because of it.
A man sits down, turning his back,
    while another murders a third—
Let me give you the son as an enemy, brother as foe,
    a man killing his father.

        " —Each mouth is full of love, of love,
            but all the loveliness is gone.

"Lawless the land which instituted law:
    destroyed is like created, lost like found,
        and what is done and what is not done are the same.
A man's property is stolen from him,
    handed to some outsider—
I give you the owner grieving, the stranger content;
    who does not take his own gets nothing.
They relinquish their goods in wordless anger
    to silence the tongue of the slanderer.
They answer the letter sent by authority—
    they answer by killing the messenger.

        " —Words fall on the heart like fire;
            yet men will not suffer a man who speaks out.

"Meager the land and many its overlords,
    wasted the wealth of its revenues;
Little the grain and large the accounting
    so that one abandons the field as it greens.

"Rê withdraws himself from mankind
    so that he shines down but fitfully —
One never knows when midday happens,
    one cannot distinguish shadows,
There is no splendor to see by
    — eyes cannot stream with tears.
He shall move in the sky like the moon,
    the rhythms of whose waning cannot be delayed;
His beams shine in the living face
    no brighter than for those who have passed on.

"Let me give you the land as a picture of sickness:
    weak-armed and strong fare the same,
        one bows to him who should offer greeting.
Let me give you the lower raised above higher:
    he who followed before leads the pack
        — one might as well be at rest in the graveyard.
The poor man shall mass riches
    while the great shall struggle to live;
It is the destitute, they eat the white bread
    while the workers work and mourn.

        " — For our homeland no more Heliopolis,
          that birthplace of every god.

"But a king shall come from the South,
    Ameny, blesséd, his name,
Son of a girl of Ta-Sety, the Southland,
    child of the palace at Hieraconpolis.

And he shall seize the White Crown of the South,
    and he shall raise up the Red of the North,
And he shall unite the Two Mighty Ones,
    let Horus and Seth be at peace, and their fellows;
And he shall gather the lands in his grasp,
    strong since the days of his swaddling clothes!
Joy shall be to the people of his time —
    for a worthy son who shall make his name
        to endure forever and forever.

"Those fallen to evil, those plotting rebellion —
    they have silenced their mouths in fear of him;
Asiatics shall fall to his sword,
    Libyans shall fall to his fire.
Rebels shall be given to him for instruction,
    the disaffected made to respect him again —
And the serpent-goddess going before him
    shall soothe surviving antagonists.

"They shall build Walls-of-the-Ruler, the fortress —
    no more Asiatics to come down into Egypt!
Let them beg for water according to custom
    to let their cattle drink.

"Justice shall rise to her throne;
    wrongdoing be utterly driven away!
How fortunate those who shall see him,
    who shall swell the train of that king!

ᗡ ᗡ ᗡ

    "The wise man shall pour a thank-offering to me
        when he sees what I have said happen."

The Testament of Amenemhat

THIS "INSTRUCTION" of a royal father to his son dates to the reigns of Amenemhat I and Senusert I of Dynasty XII in the first half of the twentieth century B.C. The old king (Amenemhat) has been slain in a palace coup and returns as a ghost (much like Hamlet's father) to explain to his royal son (Senusert) and followers just what had happened in their absence. In the course of his appearance he gives some realistic and sometimes bitter advice to his son, at the same time offering an apologia for his life. The vocabulary and poetry of this piece are especially vivid; and Amenemhat's affection for Senusert, in particular, well survives the forty centuries since the poem was composed.

The Testament of Amenemhat

Here begins the testament
        made by the Majesty of Egypt, King Sehetepibrê,
Son of the Sun, Amenemhat,
        true of voice,
That which he uttered as an accurate accounting
        to his royal son, the Lord of All,
        and which he uttered risen as a god:

"Hear what I have to say
        that you be sovereign of the Land indeed,
And rule the riverbanks of all the world,
        and reap abundance of good fortune.

"Be on your guard with underlings who never prove,
        who do not true their hearts with their intentions;
        do not be near them when you walk alone.
Fill not your heart with brothers, do not know a friend,
        nurture no intimates—there is no good in these things.
At rest, trust in your watching heart alone;
        for none are there to help a man
        when the day of trouble dawns.

"I gave to the poor and raised the humble,
        advanced the man from nowhere like the man of means;
But it was he who ate my food who mustered troops,
        the one I circled with my arms hatched plots therein,
Those clothed with my fine linen thought me dressed in weeds,
        and those perfumed with myrrh spilled out my water.

"Still-living likenesses of me, my heirs among mankind,
        make me such outcry as the world has not yet heard,
        such fighting as has never yet been seen!

Yet do not take to battle not knowing yesterday;
        good never comes to one without the truth:

"It was after dinner, night was come,
        and I had sought an hour of relaxation;
I rested on my bed, I drowsed,
        my mind began to follow after sleep—
And then there seemed a brandishing of swords, an asking for me,
        and I was furtive like a snake among the tombs.

"I woke to fighting, once my mind was back,
        and found it an assault upon the guard.
If I had quickly taken weapons in my hand,
        I would have sent the reptiles packing to their holes;
But there is no man brave at night, none who can fight alone,
        nor can good fortune fall, wanting a defender.

"And see what happened! Foul murder, while I was without you,
        before the courtiers could hear what I bequeathed you.
Now I shall never mount the throne beside you, furthering your counsel.
        I was not steeled for this! I did not think it!
        Nor could my heart conceive default by trusted
                servants.
Can it be that women marshal armies?
        And does one nurture vipers in the home?
Or loose the torrent which destroys the fields
        when one can only hurt the poor who work them?

"Harm never reared behind me since my birth,
        nor was my twin in bravery ever born!
I traveled the far South, turned back to Delta marshes,
        stood on the edges of the world and saw its contours,
Attained the outer limits of this mighty Egypt
        with my strong arm and in my many incarnations.

"It was I who brought forth grain, the grain god loved me,
       the Nile adored me from his every source;
One did not hunger during my years, did not thirst;
       they sat content with all my deeds, remembering me fondly;
       and I set each thing firmly in its place.
I bated lions, captured crocodiles;
       I conquered Nubians and brought back Medjai,
       and I made Asiatics crawl like dogs.

"I reared myself a dwelling chased with gold:
       its ceilings lapis lazuli, its walls of silver,
Its flooring sycamore, its doors of copper,
       the doorbolts were of bronze—
Made for eternity, made ready for all time;
       and now I am sole Lord, world without end.

"Many of the royal Family live here still—
       the wise affirm my words, the ignorant demur
       because they did not understand without your presence.
Senusert, royal Son, my feet are leaving;
       yet would my heart draw near, my eyes still gaze upon you.
The Family now enjoy peace and good fortune,
       and those among the Sunfolk give you praise.

"All that I did at first I interwove at last for you—
       I brought to harbor what was in my heart:
The gods are worshipped, White Crown worn by offspring of the god,
       and all is well that I began for you.

"I have descended to the Barque of Rê,
       rise to the kingship which has been since time began;
And do not act in my stead faithlessly,
       but raise the godly Images, furnish your final home,
And shield the wisdom of an upright heart
       because you always loved to have it by your side."

Two Spells

S PELLS WERE composed and recited in order to bring about desired effects by supernatural means, often with the aid of the gods. The first here translated is a love spell used by a male to secure the affections of his beloved. It appears on an ostracon dating to the Ramesside Period of the New Kingdom (ca. 1292–1070 B.C.). The second poem is from the much earlier Coffin Texts of the First Intermediate Period and the Middle Kingdom (ca. the twenty-second through the nineteenth centuries B.C.). Here the reciter seeks to obtain the breath of life from the Four Winds in order to function in the Otherworld and in order to see the face of God. There is heavy emphasis on knowing the secret names of the personages; for thereby one gains power over them.

Spell for Causing the Beloved to Follow After

Hear me, O Rê, Falcon of Twin Horizons,
                                father of gods!
Hear me, you seven Hathors
                        who weave fate with a scarlet thread!
O Hear, all you gods of heaven and earth! —

                Grant
That this girl, true child of her mother,
                        pursue me with undying passion,
Follow close on my heels
                        like a cow seeking pasture,
                like a nursemaid minding her charge,
                        like a guardian after his herd!

For if you will not cause her to love me,
        I must surely abandon the day
                        consumed to dust in the fire of my burning.

Power from the Four Winds of Heaven

These winds have been offered me by the Maidens:
The North Wind is she who caresses sea-washed islands,
        spreads wide her welcoming arms to the ends of earth,
Grows quiet at night
        to further her lover's designs each new day.
She is the breath of life, the North Wind,
        offered to me
          and through her I live.

These winds have been offered me by the Maidens:
The East Wind is she who raises the lashes of seeing,
          discloses dawn,
        makes glittering way for the footstep of God
          when he strides over eastern horizon.
Oh, let Rê hold fast to my arm,
Place me there in his field,
        at peace amid rushes,
There leave me eating and drinking forever,
        blessed by Osiris and Seth.
She is the breath of life, the East Wind,
        offered to me
          and through her I live.

These winds have been offered me by the Maidens:
This is the West Wind, brother to Ha,
        fiery lord of the Libyan desert,
      offspring and image of Iaaw,
        bird god of ancestral Lapwings,
Alive since the day of the One People
        (before ever the share became Two),
      companion still to the Land one once more.

He is the breath of life, the West Wind,
                offered to me
                        and through him I live.

These winds have been offered me by the Maidens:
This is the South Wind, African,
                        who flows from the ancient Source,
                god bringing Egypt water
                        that life be sturdy and prosper.
He is the breath of life, the South Wind,
                offered to me
                        and through him I live.

Be praised, O you Four Winds of Heaven,
                        unseen spirits of sky,
I call you each by your Name,
                        by the unspeakable Name They gave you;
And I know your manner of birth,
                once your Name appeared in the world
Back before man was conceived,
                before even gods came to be,
Before ever birds had been snared,
                before the taming of cattle,
Before the Wailer's jaws were tied shut,
                        daughter of Dawnstar,
                before ever Mind mastered Trouble—
                        possessor of heaven and earth.

I sought these Names from the Lord of Powers,
                and He it is gave them to me.
"Come, come along, to ferry the skyways together!
                I grant you to view the sky-ship,
                        embark,
                sail waves of the starry sea."

"No, no! It is I myself who fashioned a vessel
    to cross to the precinct of God;
And there, I shall launch the thousand-foot ship
    and sail to the Staircase of Fire!"

Confronting the Sun, before the bright face of God,
    may he sail to the Staircase of Fire!

The Greatness of the King

Tʜɪs ɪs one of a series of poems celebrating the power of Senusert III of Dynasty XII. Such praises of the god-king comprise one of the major kinds of ancient Egyptian literature.

The Greatness of the King

How great is the Lord of his city!
    He is exalted a thousand times over; other persons are small.
How great is the Lord of his city!
    He is a dyke which holds back the River, restraining its flood of water.
How great is the Lord of his city!
    He is a cool room which lets each man sleep until dawn.
How great is the Lord of his city!
    He is a rampart with walls of copper from Sinai.
How great is the Lord of his city!
    He is a refuge which does not lack his helping hand.
How great is the Lord of his city!
    He is a fort which rescues the fearful man from his enemy.
How great is the Lord of his city!
    He is a sunshade to help keep cool in summer.
How great is the Lord of his city!
    He is a warm dry nook in winter.
How great is the Lord of his city!
    He is the mountain which blocks the storm in a time of raging sky.
How great is the Lord of his city!
    He is Sakhmet against the enemies who test his borders.

Prayer of King Ramesses II

At the Battle of Kadesh, ca. 1285 B.C.

KING RAMESSES II, leading his troops against the Hittites at the Battle of Kadesh, finds himself alone in the face of the enemy. This passage is his prayer to his divine father, Amun, to give him aid. The poem is a mini-epic in form, presenting Ramesses as a warrior-hero. His prayer to Amun is answered.

Prayer of King Ramesses II
At the Battle of Kadesh, ca. 1285 B.C.

Then said his Majesty:

"What is this with you, my Father Amun?
    What sort of father ignores his son?
        My plans collapse without you.
Have I not gone and listened for your voice
    that I might not disobey the counsel which you gave?
—How great he is, the mighty Lord of Egypt,
    letting foreigners encroach upon his lands!—
What is on your mind?
    These Asiatics are hiding scoundrels ignorant of God!

"Have I not constructed for you many towering monuments?
    Did I not fill your temples with my spoils of war?
Did I not build for you my House of Millions of Years
    and give you all my goods as legacy?
Did I not govern for you each land entire
    in order to provide your offerings?
Did I not present to you some thirty thousand oxen
    along with many plants and flowers of sweet aroma?
Did I not turn from the good that would be mine
    in order to complete the buildings in your courtyard?
Did I not raise you mighty gates of stone
    and set their flags myself?
Did I not bring you obelisks from Abu?
    And it was I who furnished workers skilled in stone!
Did I not bring over ships from the Great Green Sea
    in order to convey to you the work of foreign lands?

"Might one consider then a small good deed
    in favor of the one who trusts himself to your good counsel?
Do good to him who counts on you;
    then he obeys you with a heart of love!

"I have cried out to you, my Father Amun,
    amidst a multitude of enemies I do not know.
The foreign lands assembled fight against me,
    I am alone, there is no other with me.
My host of infantry has gone,
    nor did a single charioteer look back at me
        as I cried out to them;
Not one heard me
    as I called to them.

"But then I found Amun mighty for me
    above a million soldiers, a hundred thousand charioteers,
More than ten thousand men, comrades and children,
    united in singleness of heart.
No, not the work of multitudes of people —
    Amun is mightier than they!
I learned these things from your own mouth, O Amun;
    and I did not exceed your counsel.

"So, I prayed at the far end of the world,
    and my voice echoed through Thebes;
And I found that Amun would come
    once I cried out to him.
He put his hand in mine
    and I was happy.
And he called as if behind me,
    'Go forward! I am with you!
        I am your Father, my hand is in yours!

I am stronger than hundreds of thousands of men!
    I am the Lord of Battle, Lover of Victory!'

"And I found that my heart was steadied,
    and my mind was filled with joy;
All I was doing turned out well,
    and I attacked like Montu!"

For a Portrait of the Queen

T HIS POEM, actually a love song, was carved into the
wall of the temple at Luxor around the middle of the
thirteenth century B.C. and commemorates Nefertari, Great Royal Wife of
King Ramesses II, the pharaoh who ruled Egypt for most of that century. There
is a charming contrast between the public situation of the poem and its loving
description of the queen.

For a Portrait of the Queen

This was a princess.

Of the line royal, lady most praiseworthy
         and a woman of charm, sweet for love,
Yet Mistress ruling two countries,
         the Twin Lands of Sedge and Papyri.

See her, her hands here shaking the sistra
         to bring pleasure to God, her father Amun.
How lovely she moves,
         her hair bound with fillets,
Songstress with perfect features,
         a beauty in double-plumed headdress,
And first among harim women
         to Horus, Lord of the Palace.

Pleasure there is in her lips' motions,
         all that she says, it is done for her gladly,
Her heart is all kindness, her words
         gentle to those upon earth.
One lives just to hear her voice.

         On this wall, by this door, she stands singing,
Great Royal Wife of the Sovereign
         (and a girl King Ramesses loved),
Consort to Power and Majesty,
         she is Queen of the Realm, Nefertari.

Hymn to Osiris

N O   G O D was more fundamental to the consciousness
of the ancient Egyptians than Osiris, god of resurrec-
tion and king of the Afterworld. Rê and Amun were equally significant; but
they played different roles as gods of creation or the cosmos, either in form
visible (Rê, the sun) or invisible (Amun, the "hidden"). The story of Osiris is
that of a benevolent king murdered through envy of his goodness, who died
and rose again, restored to life by his sister-wife, the great goddess Isis. Posthumously he became the father of a son, Horus, who avenged the evil done
his father by appeal to the tribunal of the Nine Great Gods of the universe.
Justice and the balance of things were restored by awarding Horus his rightful
inheritance, the land of Egypt. The example of Osiris assured the Egyptian
of resurrection into a happy eternal life; and in later dynasties each person
thought of himself or herself as "an osiris" who would be born again forever.
The text derives from the stela of Amenmose, who lived during Dynasty XVIII
(ca. 1550–1292 B.C.).

Hymn to Osiris

i

Turn your face gentle upon us, Osiris!

Lord of the life eternal, king of the gods,
Unnumbered the names of his protean nature,
        holy his manifold visible forms,
                hidden his rites in the temples.
First in Busiris is he, that noble spirit,
        splendid his wealth in Letopolis,
Hailed in the ancestral home of Andjeti,
        finely provided in Heliopolis;
God who remembers still
        down in the halls where men must speak true,
Heart of the inexpressible mystery,
        lord of regions under the earth,
Worshipped in white-walled Memphis, power that raises the sun,
        whose earthly form rests in Heracleopolis;
Long echo his chants in the Pomegranate nome
        where the sacred tree sprang, a perch for his soul;
Who dwells in the high Hermopolitan temple,
        most awful god in Hypselis,
Lord of forever, first in Abydos,
        yet far off his throne in the red land of death.

His tale endures in the mouths of men:
        god of the elder time,
Belonging to all mankind—
        he gave earth food,
Finest of the Great Nine,
        most fruitful among the divinities.

ii

It was for him chaos poured forth its waters
        and the north wind drove upstream;
Sky would make breeze for his nostrils
        that thereby his heart might find peace;
For his sake green things grew, and the
        good earth would bring forth its riches.
Sky and its stars obeyed him,
        for him the great gates of heaven stood open;
Praise of him thundered down southern skies,
        he was adored under northern heavens;
The circling, unfaltering stars
        wheeled near his watchful eye,
And the weary ones, who sink below seeing—
        with them was his very dwelling.

iii

And he went forth in peace
        bearing the mace of Earth, his father,
            and the Nine Great Gods gave worship;
Those in the underdark kissed ground,
        grateful dead in the desert bowed,
Gone generations joyed when they saw him,
        those seated Beyond stood in awe,
And the Two Lands united worshipped him,
        welcomed the advent of majesty.
Lordly leader, first of the eminent,
        whose kingdom endures to eternity—
His rule made kingship distinguished;
        power for good of the godhead,
Gracious and kind,
        whom to see is to love.
He made the nations revere him, that mankind might
        lift up his name before all they offered him;

Rememberer of whatever was, whether in heaven or earth,
      his mind entire in the land of forgetting;
Unending the shouts and the dancing at festival—
      rites for him of rejoicing
          done by Two Lands with one will.

iv

First-ranked of his brothers, the gods,
      noblest of the Great Nine,
He made order the length of the Riverbank,
      set a son at last on his throne,
Pride of his father, Geb,
      beloved of Nut, his mother.
With strength of the leopard he threw down the rebel,
      with powerful arm slew his opponent,
          put fear on his fallen enemy,
Reached the far borders of evil, uprooted,
      unflinching, set foot on his foe.
He inherited earth from his father,
      earned the Two Lands as their king.

v

For when Geb saw how perfect he was, he gave over his throne,
      gave him to guide the world to good fortune;
And this earth he delivered into his care—
      its waters, its air, its pastures and forage,
All of its walking creatures,
      what leaps into flight or flutters down,
Its creepers and crawlers,
      and the wild desert things—
All given as his to the son of Sky;
      and the Two Lands approved the succession.

vi

And he rose splendid, ascended the seat of his father in glory,
       like Rê when he shines from horizon;
He put dawn on the blank face of darkness,
       igniting the sun with his double plume;
And he flooded the Two Lands with well-being
       like the Sun-disk rising at day.
His gleaming crown pierced heaven,
       became a brother to stars.
And he lived and ruled, a pattern for deity—
       good king governing well—
Praised and admired by greatest gods
       while lesser divinities loved.

vii

His sister served as shield and defender,
       beat off the enemies,
Ended unspeakable mischief by power of her spell,
       golden-tongued goddess
          (her voice shall not fail),
Skilled to command,
       beneficent Isis,
          who rescued her brother.
Who searched for him
       and would not surrender to weariness,
Wandered this earth bent with anguish,
       restless until she had found him.
And she made him shade with her feathers,
       brought air by fanning her wings,
Performed the rites of his resurrection,
       moored, married, made breathe her brother,
Put life in the slackened limbs
       of the good god whose heart had grown weary.

And she took to herself his seed, grew big with the heritor,
          suckled and taught the child apart
               (his refuge not to be known),
Presented him, with his arm grown hardy,
          at Court in the broad hall of Geb.

viii

And the Nine Great Gods were glad:
          "Welcome, Horus, son of Osiris!
Whose heart shall endure, whose cry shall find justice,
          son of Isis and heir of Osiris!"
Assembled for him the Tribunal of Truth—
          Nine Gods and the Lord of the Universe—
Oh, the Lords of Truth, they gathered within there,
          the Untempted by Evil took seats in Geb's hall
To offer the legacy to its just owner
          and the kingship to whom it belonged.
And they found it was Horus, his voice spoke true:
          and they gave him the realm of his father.

ix

And he went forth bearing the mace of Geb;
          and he took the scepter of the Two Banks;
             and the crown stood firm on his head.

Allotted to him was earth, to be his possession,
          heaven and earth alike put under his care;
Entrusted to him mankind—
          nobles, and commons, and Sunfolk;
And the dear land of Egypt,
          the islands set in the northern sea,
Whatever the sun's disk circles—
          all these were given his governing—

And the good north wind, and the River, the flood,
        the plants men eat, and all that grows green.
And Nepri, Lord of the Risen Grain, he helped him
        to nurture fruits of the vital earth
So that Horus might bring on abundance,
        give it as gift to the nations.
And all mankind grew happy, hearts warmed,
        thoughts danced, and each face saw joy.

x

And they all gave thanks for his kindness:
        "How sweet is the love of him, say we;
His charm, it has ravished the heart.
        Great is the love for him in every person!"

And they offered this song for the son of Isis:

"His antagonist is down for his wrongdoing,
        since evil injures the mischief maker;
He who was hot to cause trouble,
        his deed recoils upon him
As Horus, son of Isis,
        who for him rescued his father:
            Hallowed be, and exalted, his name!
Majesty, it has taken its throne,
        Egypt's splendor is sure under law;
The highroad is safe, bypaths lie beckoning—
        how ordered the banks of the River!
Wrongdoing, it weakens,
        injustice shall all pass away!
Earth lives in peace under its Lord,
        Ma'at, Lady Truth, stands firm for her master,
            Man turns his back upon evil."

xi

"Hale be your heart, Osiris,
                you who were truly good,
                        for the son of Isis has taken the crown!
Adjudged to him is his father's kingdom
                down in the broad hall of Geb.
Rê it was uttered this; Thoth wrote it down;
                and the Grand Tribunal concurred.
Osiris, your father decreed in your favor!

                All he said has been faithfully done."

Hymn to the Nile

U N L I K E T H E other major gods of Egypt, the Nile did not have a special city or cult center for worship, and no temples were raised in his honor. Actually, the focus of the hymn is not so much the River itself as it is Hapy, the deified spirit or energy exhibited in the annual inundation, which brought fertility and abundance, and without which the civilization of Egypt could not have existed. As its inhabitants well knew, Egypt was "the gift of the Nile," and several hymns were composed in its god's honor. This piece is thought to derive from the Middle Kingdom and was possibly written by Khety in Dynasty XII (not the King Khety of *The Instruction for Merikarê*). Ancient scribes of the New Kingdom called this Khety the best of all the Egyptian writers.

Hymn to the Nile

i

May your countenance shine on us, Hapy, god of the moving River,
        who comes forth from earth
                returning to save the Black Land.
His features are hidden, dark in the daylight,
        yet the faithful find him fit subject for song.
He waters the landscape the Sun god has formed,
        giving life to every small creature,
Assuaging even the thirsty hills, far from the water's edge —
        for his is the rain, as it falls from heaven;
Loved by the waiting Earth, he nurtures the new-born grain,
        and crafts of the Fashioner flourish in Egypt.

ii

Lord of the fish, he sends wildfowl flying south,
        and no bird falls prey to the stormwind;
He fathers the barley, brings emmer to be,
        fills the gods' temples with odor of festival.
But let him be backward, then breathing falters,
        all faces grow fierce with privation;
Should the gods' primal shrines lie dry in the dust,
        men by the millions were lost to mankind.

iii

Absent, he unleashes greed to ravage the face of the land —
        famous and small wander homeless on highways;
And he baffles mankind as to when he draws near,
        for wayward he is, since the day Khnum made him.
Yet when sparkling he rises, the land stands rejoicing,
        every belly is filled with elation,

Hymn to the Nile, Stanza i

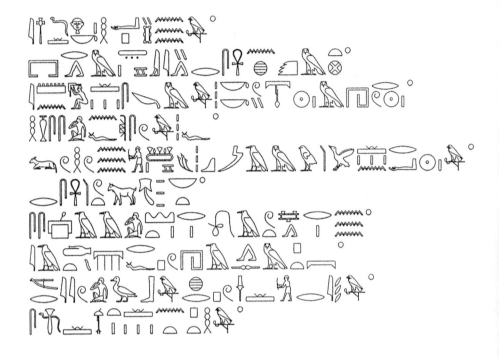

Bones of the creatures are shaken by laughter,
 teeth gleam, bared by welcoming smiles.

iv

Food bringer, rich with provisions,
 himself the author of all his good things,
Awe-striking master, yet sweet the aromas rising about him,
 and, how he satisfies when he returns! —
Transforming the dust to pastures for cattle,
 bringing forth for each god his sacrifice.
He dwells in the underworld, yet heaven and earth are his to command,
 and the Two Lands he takes for his own,
Filling the storerooms, heaping the grainsheds,
 giving his gifts to the poor.

v

He causes each kind of good wood to grow tall,
 and no one in Egypt lacks timber,
Making the ship move through force of his flow,
 so it will not settle like stone.
Yet bluffs are borne off by his fierce upsurging,
 while he himself is not seen;
He goes to his work, and will not be governed
 though they chant out the secret spells;
Man cannot know the place where he is,
 nor his grotto be spied in the writings.

vi

Flood undercuts village rises, dykes will not hold,
 sight wanders confused with no landmarks to guide it.
Yet hordes of the young join his following,
 they hail him as sovereign lord,
For he anchors the earthly rhythms, returning in his due season,
 reclaiming the Twin Lands of Sedge and Papyri:

Each eye shines with moisture by means of him,
          all are rich through his flooding kindness.

vii

Poised for his entrance, he rushes forth gladly,
          and each stranded heart floats on joy.
It was he begot Sobek, son of the Lady of Waters
          (how blessed indeed the Great Nine he fathered!) —
He foams across fields, sails over his marshland,
          impregnating earth for all men;
Yet he makes one strong while stripping another,
          nor can judgment be rendered against him;
He serves his own altars, refuses the time-honored rituals,
          endows for himself no gleaming stone temple.

viii

He illumines those who go forth in darkness —
          lighting their way with tallow of cattle;
The loom of events, it is his Power weaving,
          and no nome of the living lacks him.
He has clothed men with flax since first it was sown,
          affording Hedj-hetep help with his tasks,
Brewing resins and oils for the god of orchards
          so Ptah will have glues to fasten things tight;
He readies works of the field for Khepri to rise upon —
          there are workers themselves only because of him;
All writing belongs to the Word of god,
          and he it was supplied the papyri.

ix

He descends to the netherworld, rises again,
          Revealer, returning with news of the Mysteries;

But if listless he lies, his subjects are few —
        he kills them by letting the green world wither.
Then no better than women see Thebans,
        each man in despair destroying his gear:
No raw goods for finishing handwork,
        no cloth for fashioning clothes,
No decking out offspring of rich men,
        no shadowing beautiful eyes,
For lack of him, the trees all in ruins —
        no perfumes to linger on anyone.

x

He plants a sense of due Order deep in the hearts of mankind,
        lest men forswear the helpless among them;
In perfect accord he joins with the Great Green Sea
        nor seeks to control the sweep of its waters;
He offers each god due praise and worship
        while letting no bird fall to his desert.
There is no grasping of his hand after gold —
        for no man slakes thirst drinking money,
One cannot eat precious stone and be nourished —
        food first, let prosperity follow.

xi

Songs to the harp are begun for him,
        chanters and singers clap hands,
Troops of the young shout for joy to him,
        the irrepressible crowd is arrayed: —
For he comes! bringing riches, burnishing bright the dull land,
        renewing the color and flesh of mankind,
Fostering dreams of women with child,
        wanting hosts of the whole world of creatures.

xii

When godlike he shines amid hungry townsmen,
        by his fruits of the field are they satisfied.
He provides for the lotus its new show of blossoms,
        and all that feeds green things overflows earth;
The pastures are crowded with children—
        they have forgotten how hungry they were;
Good streams through the streets and squares,
        the length of the land frisks and flowers.

xiii

Hapy rides high, and thanksgiving is offered him:
        for him long-horned cattle are slaughtered,
For him the festival meal prepared,
        fowl are made fat for him,
Lions trapped out on the desert,
        debts of kindness repaid him;
And to each god they make offering
        just as·is done for Hapy:
Incense, birds, beasts big and small—all are given;
        and down in his cave Hapy stirs, irresistible.
Yet not in the underworld shall his name be known,
        nor can the very gods reveal it.

xiv

All men honor the Nine Great Gods,
        but They stand in awe of that deity
Who aids his son, divine Lord of All,
        in greening the banks of the Nile.
O hidden god, be it well with you! may you flourish, and return!
        Hapy, river spirit, may you flourish and return!

Come back to Egypt, bringing your benediction of peace,
        greening the banks of the Nile;
Save mankind and the creatures, make life likely,
        through the gift of all this your countryside!
O hidden god, be it well with you! may you flourish, and return!
        Hapy, Lord of Egypt, may you flourish and return!

Hymn to the Rising Sun
Ch. XV, Pap. of Ani

PROBABLY THE richest genre of ancient Egyptian literature was the hymn or prayer to one or another of the gods. This, from the Papyrus of Ani, which contains one of the most extensive compilations of the New Kingdom Book of the Dead, celebrates the course across the sky of the sun god, Rê.

Hymn to the Rising Sun
Ch. XV, Pap. of Ani

Adoration of Rê in his rising from the horizon
until he comes to rest in life.
Words spoken by the osiris, the scribe Ani:

Be praised, O Rê, in your rising,
    Atum-Horakhty!
Let your perfections be worshipped with my eyes,
    and let your sunlight come to be within my breast.
May you proceed in your own peace in the Night Barque,
    your heart rejoicing in a following breeze within the Day Barque.
How delightful is the crossing of the skies among the peaceful dead
    with all your enemies fallen!
The unwearying stars give praise to you,
    the indestructible stars adore you—
You who go to rest in the horizon of the Western Mountains,
    beautiful as the Sun each day,
        beautiful, enduring, as my Lord.

In Praise of Amun

THIS, LIKE the preceding piece, celebrates one of the great gods, Amun. Unlike Rê, who shines from the sky, Amun is here seen as hidden and inward; and his petitioner presumes a close relationship with the god.

In Praise of Amun

A pilot who knows the waters, that is Amun,
    a steering oar for the [helpless],
One who gives food to the one who has not,
    who helps the servant of His house to prosper.

I do not take myself a great man as protector,
    nor do I mingle with the men of means;
I do not place my portion under the strong arm
    of someone wealthy in a noble household.

My Lord is my protector,
    I know His strength;
He aids with ready arm and caring look,
    and, all alone, is powerful—

Amun, who knows what kindness is
    and hears the one who cries to Him;
Amun, King of the Gods,
    strong Bull who glories in His power.

Lament to Amun

THIS IS a prayer found on a New Kingdom papyrus dating to ca. 1200 B.C. The writer describes a world gone wrong and asks God to help him escape it.

Lament to Amun

Come to me, Father Amun,
        protect me in this bitter year of confrontation.
God shines in the sun; yet he will not shine,
        winter crowds hard upon summer.
Months happen backwards;
        disheveled hours lurch drunken by.
Those cut down in high places cry out to you, Amun;
        the beaten in alleyways seek you;
And the new generation at the breasts of its nurses
        wails, "Give us our Lebensraum, Father!"
God find in his heart to return, bringing peace,
        bringing air, the clean breeze before him.
Or let him grow me the wings of protection
        to soar like his sky-ship high beyond earth.

        —These words came on the poisoned air,
Spoken by herdsmen in fields and marshes,
        by those who beat clothes on the banks of the river,
By district police deserting their precincts,
        by horned beasts on our burning deserts.

The Tale of Sinuhe

THIS TALE is considered by many Egyptologists to be the finest piece of literature to survive from ancient Egypt. It is the story of a trusted courtier who ran away from an attempted coup, escaping into voluntary exile in Syria-Palestine, where he lived out most of his life alienated from his Egyptian roots. The tale shows him slowly working his way back to self-esteem and eminence. Toward the end of his life he is able to return to Egypt where he is warmly welcomed by his king and the royal family whose servant he had been. A good many of the fundamental values of ancient Egyptian civilization are embodied in this narrative. The now-anonymous author conceived and executed the poem so splendidly that, on the basis of present evidence, he can rightly be called the Shakespeare of ancient Egypt. The tale is from Dynasty XII in the twentieth century B.C.

The Tale of Sinuhe

i

The man of ancient family, chief of his town,
>who bore the goddess' seal for Lower Egypt, Only Friend,
Senior overseer of waterways,
>viceroy for Asian lands,
Trusted adviser to the King, one he esteemed,
>the courtier Sinuhe.
>>It is he who speaks:

I was a good and faithful servant of my Lord,
>attendant in the harim
>>of the Lady of noble blood, most highly favored,
King's Wife of Senusert
>seated as consort on the throne,
Daughter of Amenemhat
>in the city of Qa-nefer,
>>Neferu,
>>>gone long ago to bliss.

ii

Regnal Year Thirty,
>Third Month of the Inundation, Day Seven,
Day of Ascension: god mounts toward his last horizon,
>King of the Sedge and the Bee, Sehetep-ib-Rê,
That he might soar to heaven, be one with the Sun,
>flesh of the god mingling with God who made him.
The Royal City is silent, the heart without consolation,
>the Great Paired Gates are sealed;
Courtiers crouch, head bent on knee,
>the people groan with grief.

Now see the situation: his Majesty passed on
          and the army west in the Libyan desert,
His eldest son commanding,
          the beneficent god, Crown Prince Senusert.
Sent to punish barbarian lands,
          destroying all who would live among Libyans,
He was now returning with what he had taken —
          doomed slaves from those desert tribes
              and unnumbered cattle and livestock.

The council of royal advisers (the Palace Companions)
          sent word to the western side
In order to let the king's son know
          what had transpired in his father's chamber.
The envoys found him upon the march,
          having come under cover of darkness.
Not a moment at all did he linger:
          the Falcon, he flew with his followers
             never letting his army know.

iii

Somehow word reached the King's other sons
          (those with the prince on this expedition);
And Someone called one son aside in the dark
          while I, I was standing right there —
I heard his very voice while he spoke treason
          and I on the rising ground close by!
My heart then hung undone, fear paralyzed my arms,
          a shuddering shook my body.
But I made good retreat, and scurried off
          to find fit place to hide,
Cowering down within some bushes
          which screened the road from the runaway.

Then I continued on upstream,
        for I hardly meant to stop by the Residence:
I feared civil disorder—
        nor would I long outlive the late King.
I wandered the Maaty Canal, crossing it nearby Sycamore,
        and touched down on Sneferu's Island;
I spent the day resting there at the edge of the cultivation
        and set out bright the next dawn,
Startling a man standing square in my path
        who bowed low with respect, for he was afraid.
At last the dinner hour came on,
        and I had gained the landing near Cattleford.

I crossed the Nile in a rudderless boat
        blown on the breath of the west wind
And faded from sight east of the Quarry
        moving south of the Lady of Red Peak.
Then I offered the road to my feet, turning north,
        and skirted Walls-of-the-Ruler,
Built to ward off vile Asiatics
        and discourage bedouin wanderers.
I took to crouching down in the brush
        for fear of seeing the sentry
                who was up on the wall, on duty,
        and continued on and on through the night.

Day dawned, and I had reached Peten,
        alit on an isle of the Great Salt Sea.
Thirst fell, it drove me on;
        I was choking, my throat clogged with dust;
And I said to myself, "So this is the taste of death!"
        and steadied my heart for the end.
But then I heard the lowing of cattle
        and I saw . . . blest Asiatics!

The sheikh of that crew knew me
   (a man who often went down into Egypt),
So he gave me water to drink
   and afterward boiled me milk.
I returned with him to his bedouin people,
   and splendid it was, all they did for me!

Land gave me to land
   once I set out for Byblos, cutting the ties behind;
Then I turned east toward the Qedem hills,
   staying a year and a half in that region.

iv

Then Amunenshi fetched me away
   (he was ruler of Upper Retenu),
     saying,
"You would do well with me
   and you would hear the accents of Egypt."
He broached this knowing my reputation
   (he had already heard of my skill);
And native Egyptians vouched for me
   of those who were with him there.

Then he went on,
   "How in the world have you come this far?
     Has something occurred at the palace?"

And I replied,
   "Sehetep-ib-Rê. Gone to his last horizon.
     One cannot know what happens after."
And I added (wide of the truth)
   that I had returned with the army from Libya:
"They told it to me, and my heart shook—
   my heart drove me out on the wide ways of flight.

I was not spat upon,
            nor did they lay charges against me.
I know not what brings me here to this land;
            it was a miracle of God—
As if a Delta man should find himself up-River
            or a bewildered marshman in the Nubian sand!"

At that he mused before me,
            "What will poor Egypt do
                        lacking his help, that late and splendid god?
Respect for him pervades the world
            like fear of our Great Lady in a year of plague."

Thus he said, and thus I answered him,
            "Surely his son is risen to the palace,
                        taking, himself, his father's heritage:

v

"For he is a god indeed, without an equal,
            no other came to be before him,
Lord of wisdom, wise in counsel,
            potent in commanding words;
Envoys come and go to do his bidding,
            and he it is subdues the foreign lands:
The father stays behind within the palace,
            the son reporting: what is ordered, it is done.

"He is a warrior too, of royal deeds,
            brave, with no likenesses among mankind.
He can be seen in splendor scattering alien hordes
            once he has joined the heat of battle;
He forces down the bow, unnerves the hand—
            rebels cannot muster strength for opposition;

He is hawk-eyed, skull-splitting—
        none make a stand near him.

"Wide-striding, he shoots down the coward runaway—
        and there's an end to all who show their heels.
Unflinching under pressure of assault,
        he faces forward—never turns *his* back!
Steadfast he eyes the surging multitude
        nor lets the villains gain his center;
Eager, he harries the Easterners,
        exulting, herds the barbarians.

"Let him but seize the shield to enter battle,
        he never need do twice the deed of devastation!
There are none who escape his arrow,
        none who can draw his bow.
Foreign cohorts flee before him
        as from the vengeance of the Mighty Goddess;
Fighting in his absence ends—
        he cannot linger for the stragglers.

"Yet he is dearly loved, deep in the people's affection,
        taking the throne as his own with their blessing:
His citizens treasure him more than their own flesh,
        set him above their own god.
They pass down the roadways singing with joy in him
        now he is king;
But he took this land while still with his mother,
        his eye on the kingdom before he was born.

"He shall make Egypt's children be many and multiply,
        yet he is one, the One given of God.
Egypt enjoys all he inherited—
        now he shall broaden her far-flung borders:

He shall go forth and take the lands of the south,
                never think twice of the northern nations;
He is sent by God to smite Asiatics
                and grind the desert tribes into dust. . . .

"Write him! Make sure he knows your name!
                And do not weigh the distance to his Majesty
                        that he may help you as his father did.
He cannot fail to aid
                a country asking his protection."

Amunenshi then replied,
                "Egypt surely will be well;
                        she knows his guiding hand. . . .
But you are here, so you shall stay with me;
                and I shall do you good."

vi

And so he set me down, honored among his children,
                and wed me to his oldest girl,
And let me have my choice of all his districts
                picked from the very best of what was his
                        up at the border with the neighboring country:
                it was a splendid land, called Yaa.

Figs were there, along with grapevines:
                wine flowed more plentiful than water.
A land of honey, endless with olives,
                and fruits of every kind bent down its branches.
And there was barley there, and emmer;
                the land lay well, luxuriant with livestock.
Greatness and power indeed reached out to me
                because of his affection.

Then he set me to rule the people
       in that choicest and best of places.
They furnished me food day by day
       and wine was a daily pleasure,
With always cooked meat or roast duck
       or dishes of desert game.
They snared for me and they fished for me,
       swelling the catch of my own greyhounds;
And they filled me with numberless sweets,
       with milk and abundance of baked goods.

I spent untold years there;
       my sons grew to powerful men
         each leading his own people.
The envoy speeding north or south toward home —
       he stopped awhile with me.
Indeed, all mankind knew my courtesy:
       I gave the thirsty one to drink,
I set the lost upon his way,
       I succored him whom thieves had wrecked.

Now, the Asiatics fell to insurrection
       baiting rulers of the upland counties;
         and I was totally opposed to all their scheming.
So my good Lord of Retenu,
       he had me spend more years
Acting as marshal of his forces;
       and each hill district flocked to me for refuge.

Then I swept down upon those Asian hordes,
       and doom descended on their wells and pastures.
I took their cattle,
       carried off their farmers;

I seized their harvests
      and I killed their people
With my strong arm, with my bow,
      my tactics and my skillful strategy.

I stood there splendid in my master's heart, for he esteemed me;
      and now he knew that I was brave.
He made me foremost among all his offspring
      having seen my strong arm prosper.

vii

Then came a doughty chief of Retenu
      to taunt me, goad me from my tent;
He was supreme, a champion without contenders,
      since he had overmanned them, every one.
He said he wanted single combat with me
      fully expecting he would lay me low,
Intending to carry off my cattle
      under the evil urging of his tribe.

That other lord, my chief, he begged a word with me —
      I protesting that I did not know the man:
"I am certainly no friend of his
      that I could wander free in his encampment!
Does it look like I could force his private chamber
      having breached his wall and stormed his citadel?
He is beside himself because he sees me
      happily embarked on your affairs.

"Surely I am like the lead bull of a roving band
      chanced in the middle of a settled herd:
The hero of the native stock attacks him
      while other longhorns nudge and menace.

Is ever man of humble origin esteemed
             in the capacity of master?
No desert wanderer joins with a Delta farmer! —
             and who would grow papyrus in the mountains?
Is there a bull aching to test the champion
             who dares to sound retreat
                          for fear he might not equal him?
If this chief's lust be all to fight,
             let him speak out what weighs upon his mind.
Can God be ignorant of what this man has planned?
             The question is, my good lord, How can *we* know?"

I spent the night testing my bow,
             cutting and truing arrows,
Made some practice passes with my dagger
             and readied all my gear.

Day dawned; all Retenu was come,
             for they had irritated and inflamed its peoples
And gathered districts sympathetic to their cause —
             oh, they indeed had staged this confrontation!

He made his entrance there where I was standing,
             for I had made myself available to him.
The thoughts of all burned fierce with anguish for me,
             women and men murmured in alien tongues;
Each heart had pity on me, asking,
             "Is there another hero able to do battle with him,
To stand against his shield, his axe,
             his armful of such deadly missiles?"

Then I strode forth amidst his flying weaponry
             which I let pass me harmless by:
His arrows bit thin air,
             one following the other uselessly.

And then he made his sally
       fully intending there to have me dead;
He neared me and I shot him,
       my arrow bedding in his neck;
He groaned, he fell upon his face,
       and I dispatched him with his battle-axe.

I roared my victory shout over his prostrate form
       while each vile Asian howled,
Gave thanks to Montu, Lord of Battle,
       while his inept supporters wept for him.
Our friend and master, Amunenshi—
       he wrapped me in his arms.

At that I carried off this hero's goods
       and took his herds:
What he had planned to do to me
       I did to him.
I made my own whatever filled his tent
       and stripped his campsite bare.

Honor and power and glory were mine from that deed;
       only the far horizon bounded my heaped-up riches;
          droves of my cattle, uncounted, covered the hills—
       thus does God ever act toward a man of good will:
He does not nurse anger against one
       who has wandered astray to the wrong land.

          And this day proves His heart is washed clean!

viii

"A fugitive once fled his neighborhood;
       Now word of me thunders back home.
One trusted to stay once crept away hungry;
       today I give bread to my neighbor.

The Tale of Sinuhe, lines 321–330

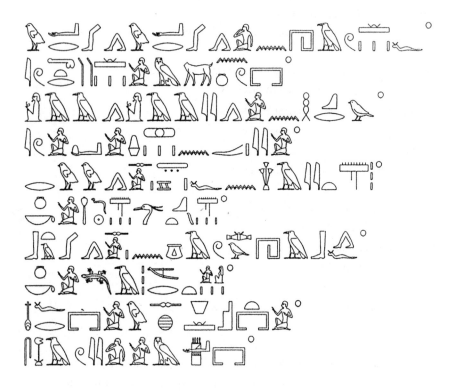

A man abandoned his own land in nakedness;
   I am one who shines in fine linen.
A man went himself for want of a messenger;
   I am a man rich in servants.
Splendid my tent here, and wide my domain —
   but I still have dreams of the palace.

"Lord of all gods, who ordered this flight,
   I pray you send me home!
Surely you will let me see
   the place my heart would dwell.
What better than my body's union
   with that earth where I was born?
Come, seek me out, that a good deed may be done,
   and let God give me peace.

"And may He act likewise
   to dignify the end of one He has afflicted;
May His heart pity one He has condemned
   to let life leak away on arid hills.
Is it today indeed that He is reconciled?
   Let Him then hear the prayer of one afar!
Let the sojourner cease to range the land of his exile;
   let him go back to the country whence God brought him.

"And may the King of Egypt be at peace with me
   that I may live within the heartland of his mercy,
And greet my Lady who is in his palace,
   and hear tidings of her children.
Then would my very self grow young again!
   For now old age is come,
And misery, alone it drives me on;
   my eyelids fall, my arms are heavy,
    feet fail to follow the exhausted heart.

"O God, be near me for the final journey
            that they may guide me to the City of Forever
                        to follow faithfully the Mistress of Us All.
Then would she tell me it is well with all her children,
            that she will while away eternity with me."

ix

At last it reached his Majesty's attention —
            He of the Sedge and the Bee, King Kheper-ka-Rê —
                        about the state that my affairs were in.
And his Majesty sent such a message to me —
            accompanied by largesse of the Crown —
As warmed the heart of this his loyal subject
            like that of any ruler of a foreign country;
And each prince and princess in the palace with him
            made sure I heard their news.

                Copy of the order brought to this loyal subject
                        concerning his return to Egypt:

"The Horus, Life of the Dynasty,
            Two Ladies, Life of the Dynasty,
                        Golden Horus, Life of the Dynasty,
He of the Sedge and the Bee, King Kheper-ka-Rê,
            Son of the Sun, Senusert,
                        alive through worlds and time —
The Order of the King for my servant, Sinuhe:

"Item. This edict of the King is brought you
            to comment on your transmigration of the lands
                        which go forth east from Qedem to the hills:

"Land gives you to land
            goaded by phantoms in your fevered brain.

What have you done that one should act against you?
            You did not blaspheme that your words should drive you off;
Nor did you ill-speak in the hall of elders
            that your phrases should rise up to haunt you.
This foolish notion, it made you leave your senses! —
            nothing like that was ever in my heart against you.

"She, your Heaven in the palace, lives here still
            and flourishes today;
Her canopy of love is spread like sky, protecting earth;
            her children prosper in the audience chamber.
Now, be assured to have whatever they will give you
            that you may live henceforth on their affection.

"Make your return to Egypt
            to see once more the home wherein you grew,
To kiss your native earth before the towering Twin Doors,
            be reunited with my loyal Friends.

"By now old age is come upon you,
            manhood cut loose and drifts away;
So think today upon the day of burial,
            your passage into light:

"You shall be granted days of darkness with sweet oils,
            a linen shroud woven by gentle Taiyt's hands;
For you they slowly step the last cortege
            upon that day of mooring, union with the earth:
The coffin all of gold, the mask of heaven's blue,
            the very sky above you caught in the covered shrine;
Oxen draw and singers sing as they precede you,
            the dance for those at rest is danced at your last door;
For you they consecrate the funeral banquet
            and sacrifice is made upon your altars;

Your pillars rise, cut from the fine white limestone,
        close to the very bosom of my Family.

"No death of yours shall be on foreign soil,
        nor shall mere Asiatics make you earth;
Never shall you lie wrapped in a sheepskin
        that such might serve as your enclosure wall.
Death is duration longer than wandering this world;
        have care for your eternal body, and come home!"

x

This document arrived
        while I was standing there among my people.
It was read out to me,
        and I threw myself upon the ground
And gathered dust of earth,
        strewing it freely on my breast.
Then I strode back and forth through my encampment
        exulting, shouting out, and saying:
"How can this be done for a mere servant
        whose heart has gone astray to alien lands?
O, wonderful indeed the clemency of him
        who saves me from the hand of death.
It is your august Self, O King, that lets me make an end,
        my limbs at rest at home."

xi

Copy of the reply to this royal Edict:

Sinuhe, Servant of the Palace, says:

"With the utmost goodwill and submission
        regarding the matter of this exodus
            made by your loyal subject in his foolishness.

My greetings to you, beneficent god, Lord of the Two Lands,
   beloved of Rê and favorite of Montu, Lord of Thebes.

"May Amun, Lord of the Throne of the Two Lands,
   and Sobek-Rê, Horus, and Hathor,
Atum with his Ennead of gods,
   and Sopdu, Neferbau, Semseru, the Eastern Horus,
The Mistress of the Underworld (may she protect your brow),
   the convocation of old deities upon the waters,
And Min, and Horus of foreign lands,
   and the Great Goddess, Mistress of Punt,
And Nut, the Elder Horus, Rê,
   and all the gods of Egypt and the Green Sea Islands—

"May They put breath of life into your nostrils,
   may They enrich you with their gifts,
And may They offer you eternity without an end
   and infinity unbounded.
May fear of you reverberate among the nations,
   and may all those beneath the round sun bow.

"This is the supplication of a servant to his Royal Master
   who can sustain him in the West:
The Lord of Understanding, who knows the common lot—
   he sees amid the awful majesty of court
How this humbled servant fears to state his plea
   as when there is a matter of grave moment to report.

"But the great god, image of Rê,
   himself makes wise the man who serves him;
And your loyal subject has in hand a small suggestion
   that One might take for his consideration:
Your Majesty is Horus, who seizes what he will—
   victorious your arms against all nations;

So, let your Majesty command
   that this your servant bring you back the prince of Qedem,
The chieftain of the Iawesh, south of Keshu,
   and the leader of the two Phoenician coastlands.
These are kings whose names are justly famous
   come into prominence with high regard for you
(There is no need to mention Retenu,
   for it belongs to you like your own greyhounds).

"As for this flight made by your loyal subject:
   I did not plan it out beforehand,
     it never crossed my mind;
I did not fabricate or nurse it,
   nor do I know what tore me from the Throne.
It was like the twistings of a dream —
   as if a Delta man should find himself up-River
     or a bewildered marshman in the Nubian sand.

"I was not fearful; no one followed me;
   I did not hear a whisper of reproach;
Nor was my name proscribed by edict of the marshal
   so that vile worms should be the judges of my body.
But yet my feet moved fast, my feelings mastered me;
   and God, who destined flight, thus drove me on.
I was not ever one to disobey —
   a good man holds in awe the customs of his country;
And Rê has set the fear of you throughout the world,
   dread of you pervades each foreign nation.

"I beg you, take me home!
   save me from all this!
For it is you who clothe this far horizon,
   the very sun-disk shines because of you;

The water in the streams, its moisture is your love;
        the wind of heaven, its very breath your speaking.

"This loyal subject shall pass power to my fledglings
        whom I have gotten in this place:
Homecoming it shall be, as offered to your servant;
        and may your Majesty do as you will.
One lives upon the breath of your dispensing,
        beloved of Rê, of Horus, and of Hathor;
Your very nostrils, they signify our riches,
        O you whom Montu, Lord of Thebes eternal, loves."

xii

They let me spend a day in Yaa
        transferring my possessions to my offspring;
My eldest son was set to lead my people,
        and all my property left in his hand—
My serfs, my many herds,
        my vines, and all my orchards.

So then this servant journeyed south toward home,
        halting at Fort Horusways;
And the commander there, who led the border watch,
        forwarded a message to the Residence
            in order that the King might be informed.

His Majesty dispatched the Minister of Planters,
        a skillful man devoted to the royal House;
And heavy-laden ships came after him
        bringing largesse of the Crown
Meant for those Asiatics who returned with me
        conducting me to Horusways.
I said good-bye to each of them by name
        while each gift-bearing servant did them honor.

Then I took to hoisting sail—
        with beer and baked provisions by my side—
          until I reached the wharf at home.

xiii

Next day the dawn came early to the earth,
        and summons came for me—
Ten men arriving, ten men going forth
        escorting me in triumph to the palace.
I offered head to ground before the statues of the Children
        which towered in the gateway, greeting me.
Courtiers attending in the outer hall
        showed me directly to the audience chamber.

I found his Majesty upon the Throne of Egypt
        in the throne room all of silvered gold.
Really there, at last, before him,
        I stretched myself full length upon the floor;
But then my foolish brain turned witless in his presence,
        just as this god was offering warm welcome.
I was a man seized in the grip of darkness—
        my bird-soul flown, my limbs unstrung;
My heart, no longer was it in my body
        so that I might distinguish life from death.

Then said his Majesty to an attendant courtier,
        "Raise him. Let him speak with me."
And then he said, "Well, well, you have come home,
        done wandering the weary world since your departure!
I see the marks of time etched on your body;
        you have grown old.
When death must come, your rites shall not be wanting—
        your burial shall never be by bedouin tribes.

Now, deprecate yourself no longer:
　　　　you spoke no treason; your name is honored here."

But still I was afraid of punishment
　　　　and answered with the answer of a frightened man,
"What is it I have said, my Lord?"
　　　　Then I could speak to it.
It was no deed of mine;
　　　　it was the hand of God:
Fear surged throughout my body
　　　　as if to force a flight divinely ordered. . . .
"But let that be.
　　　　　　　　I stand here in your presence;
　　　　to you my life belongs;
　　　　　　　　and may your Majesty do with me what you will."

Then he had the royal Family ushered in,
　　　　and his Majesty said to the Queen,
"Look, here we have Sinuhe
　　　　come back pure Semite, transformed into an Asian."

At that she uttered an astounded, "No!"
　　　　and the Children all put forth a mock-believing gasp,
Exclaiming to his Majesty,
　　　　"Surely it is not he, our sovereign Lord?"
　　　　　　　　The King, "It surely is."

Then the princesses put on their beads of supplication
　　　　and with scepters and their sistra in their hands
　　　　　　　　made presentation of a song to please his Majesty:

"Your state is more than royal, O King,
　　　　shining with the glory of the Queen of Heaven.
The Golden One gives life unto your nostrils,
　　　　and the Lady of the Stars protects you;

White Crown travels north, and Red fares south,
   joined in everlasting union in your Person;
     the Serpent rears herself upon your brow.

"You have delivered humblest men from evil,
   gratifying Rê, Lord of our Land:
     praises to you, as to the Mistress of Us All!
Lower your bow, unstring your arrow;
   give breath to one who is in need of air!
Grant us this special gift
   in favor of our errant guide, Son of the Northwind,
     this bedouin born in our beloved Land.
He ran away for fear of you,
   he left the land in terror of you;
And yet no face should pale at seeing yours,
   no fear unman the eye which looks to you."

And then his Majesty replied, "He shall not fear henceforth
   that he should falter so from terror.
He shall have rank as royal Friend among my counselors,
   be placed within the inmost circle of the court.
Proceed now to the dressing chamber
   to be of service to him."

Oh, what a Coming Forth it was for me that day —
   it was like resurrection — out of that royal hall!
The Children offered me their arms
   and then we went, together, out the Double Doors.

xiv

I stayed at a prince's estate amid splendors long lost to me:
   a cool reception hall, scenes of the life hereafter,
Masterpieces from the Treasury,
   soft-woven garments, and perfumes of delicate fragrance.

Counselors the King esteemed lived in the rooms,
           and every servant went about his duties.

They made the years fall from my body:
           I was taken and sheared, and my hair combed,
And a heavy load was given to the sandy hills—
           the cast-off livery of a desert wanderer;
I was appareled in the finest linen,
           anointed with the sweetest-smelling oils,
                and put to rest at night upon a real bed.
I bequeathed the sand to those who lived in it
           and the oil of tree to him who smelled of it.

I received a nobleman's plantation
           as befitting one who ranked as Royal Friend.
A company of expert craftsmen readied it,
           and all its woodwork was restored like new;
Food was sent me from the palace
           three and even four times every day—
                not counting what the royal Children gave.
           And not one moment did these wonders cease!

There was made for me a pyramid of stone
           built in the shadow of the royal tomb.
The god's own masons hewed the blocks for it,
           and its walls were portioned out among them;
The draftsman and the painter drew in it,
           the master sculptor carved;
The overseer of workmen at the tombs
           criss-crossed the length of Egypt on account of it.
Implements and furniture were fitted in its storeroom
           and all that would be needful brought within;
Servants for my Spirit were appointed,
           a garden was laid out above,

And tended fields ran downward to the village—
   just as is ordered for a nearest Friend.
My statue was all brushed with burnished gold,
   its kilt set off with silver.

It was his Majesty who did all this for me.
   No simple man has ever had so much.
And I enjoyed the sunshine of his royal favor
   until my day of mooring dawned.

From *The Leiden Hymns*

THIS CYCLE of poems appears on a papyrus dated to the fifty-second regnal year of Ramesses II, ca. 1227 B.C. The hymns, thus, are from this period or somewhat earlier. In them we see a culmination of ancient Egyptian theology as it developed the concept of one preeminent god, the creator, all-powerful, all-encompassing, god of all lands and peoples, and one who can appear in a multitude of forms or incarnations, including those of the other Egyptian gods. God is called "Amun" or "Amun-Rê"; but as we read the poems, we realize that the poet-theologian who composed these pieces is expressing the mystery of the One God. He moves in unfathomable ways and takes many forms to human comprehension—as the various poems demonstrate; but though He is hidden from human sight, He is indeed the ultimate godhead, God alone.

The Leiden Hymns

IX

The Nine Great Gods are come from the waters,
    gathered to worship the dayspring of Majesty,
Lord of Lords, who made himself God out of nothing,
    Lord of all deities, He is the Lord.

And those who must sleep and awaken, He shines for them too
    to brighten their faces in visible form:
His eyes glow kindly, His ears are listening,
    and each naked creature is clothed in His light.

Sky turns to gold, turquoise the primeval waters,
    the Southland is lapis lazuli blue
      as He rises shining upon them;
Gods of the old days marvel, their temples lie open,
    even late man peeps out and wonders.

Trees sway, nod and bow before Him,
    look to the one source, arms wide with blossoms;
The scaly ones flash in the water,
    bold from their hidden crannies for love of Him;
Small beasts are gay in His sight,
    birds flutter and run with stretched wings.

The creatures most truly know Him
    at this hour of His rising beauty —
    life itself is to see Him each day;
They lie in His hand, signed in His own hieroglyphic,
    and no god but God breaks the seal of their love.

There are none who can live without Him;
  He is indeed Great God,
        Power that moves all deity.

The Leiden Hymns

X

The legend of Thebes exceeds any city.
>   In the Beginning
>   hers were the waters and dry land;
Then sands came to mark off fields,
>   to form her foundations on that high hill
>   back when the world came to be;
And then there were faces of men
>   to establish the cities, each with its calling;
And all have names after their natures
>   by order of Thebes, God's Eye over Egypt.

The Majesty of Thebes came down as His salvation
>   to draw the world, through her, to the Spirit of God,
Pleased to dwell by the waters of Asheru
>   in the likeness of Sakhmet, Mistress of Egypt.
How strong she is! without contender,
>   she honors her name as Queen of the Cities.
Sharp-sighted, keen as God's protector,
>   Right Eye of Rê,
>   disciple facing her Lord,
Bright with the splendor of God,
>   wise upon her high throne,
>   she is Most Holy of Places,
>   a mecca the world cannot parallel.

Each city stirs into life at the breath of invisible God,
>   burns to be great. Like Thebes:
>   hers is the light of perfection.

The Leiden Hymns

XX

How splendid you ferry the skyways,
                       Horus of Twin Horizons,
The needs of each new day
                       firm in your timeless pattern,
Who fashion the years,
                       weave months into order —
Days, nights, and the very hours
                       move to the gait of your striding.

Refreshed by your diurnal shining, you quicken,
                       bright above yesterday,
Making the zone of night sparkle
                       although you belong to the light,
Sole one awake there
                       —sleep is for mortals,
Who go to rest grateful:
                       your eyes oversee.
And theirs by the millions you open
                       when your face new-rises, beautiful;
Not a bypath escapes your affection
                       during your season on earth.

Stepping swift over stars,
                       riding the lightning flash,
You circle the earth in an instant,
                       with a god's ease crossing heaven,
Treading dark paths of the underworld,
                       yet, sun on each roadway,

You deign to walk daily with men.

              The faces of all are upturned to you,
As mankind and gods
            alike lift their morningsong:
"Lord of the Daybreak,
             Welcome!"

The Leiden Hymns

XXX

The harpoon is deep in Apophis, the Evil,
                      he falls by the sword;
            and those who chose war are huddled for slaughter—
Death cuts the hearts of God's demon enemies,
            who groan as outlaws,
                    apostate forever.
He has ordered the remnant sacrificed
               to cripple the power of the dark Adversary
                  that God's own self be secure.

Unharmed is He in His midship chapel!
                    the holy Light shines still!
He has ridden the waves unscathed
              and rebels are no more!
The sun-ship of infinite journeys
               still sails on course through the sky,
            her godly crew cheering,
               their hearts sweet with victory.
Down is the great Antagonist,
            bane of the Lord of Creation;
         no partisan of his is found
               either in heaven or earth!

Sky, Thebes, Heliopolis, Underworld—
            their peoples are proud of their conquering god,
For they see Him strong in his sunrise epiphany
            robed in beauty and victory and power.
It is day!
     You have won, Amun-Rê!
             Gone the dark children of Enmity,
                    dead by the sword.

The Leiden Hymns

XL

God is a master craftsman;
                     yet none can draw the lines of His Person.
Fair features first came into being
                     in the hushed dark where He mused alone;
He forged His own figure there,
                     hammered His likeness out of Himself—
All-powerful one (yet kindly,
                     whose heart would lie open to men).

He mingled His heavenly god-seed
                     with the inmost parts of His being,
Planting His image there
                     in the unknown depths of His mystery.
He cared, and the sacred form
                     took shape and contour, resplendent at birth!
God, skilled in the intricate ways of the craftsman,
                     first fashioned Himself to perfection.

The Leiden Hymns

LXX

God loosens the knot of suffering, tempers disease,
　　　　physician who cures without ointments;
Clear-sighted, He unclouds the darkening vision,
　　　　opens His hidden nature to men.
He will save whom He loves, though one walk in the underworld,
　　　free from the debt due fate
　　　　　　as His heart, in wisdom, determines.

To Amun are eyes, and ears as well:
　　　　face guarding every way for one He loves;
He hears the entreaty of any who cry to Him,
　　　　come in an instant to whoever summons Him
　　　　　　the distance no matter how far.
He can lengthen a life or wreak havoc within it,
　　　offer wealth beyond fated measure
　　　　　to that man blessed by His love.
He is a water spell: His Name hovers high —
　　　God's wings span the waters of Chaos;
No power at all to Death the Crocodile
　　　when one calls on His Name.

Winds of the deep contend, a withering storm veers nigh —
　　　yet eased a man's end by remembering Him:
Spell-binding such speech at the moment of truth
　　　when man meets death face to face;
And breezes are soft for who calls upon God —
　　　He rescues the wind- and wave-weary.

For God is a god of mercy, mild in His dealing, fond;
His children are all who bow to His lordship—
upraised to the everpresence of God.
Sufficient is He above any
when housed in the human heart,
His Name alone
more potent than numberless deities.
He protects what is good in the world,
ready to take to Himself any who falter behind;
there are none to oppose Him.

The Leiden Hymns

LXXX

The Eight Great Gods were your first incarnation
   to bring to perfection this cosmos.
     You were the alone;
Secret your image from even oldest divinities:
   you had hidden yourself as Amun from faces of gods.

You entered your form as Ta-tenen, and earth rose from chaos
   bearing the primal deities back in your elder time;
Erect grew your charms as Kamutef,
   life force, lusty son of his mother;
You withdrew to the midst of heaven, and distance was born,
   endured in the sun, forming time,
Returned as the father gods, and they begat sons,
   beginning the generations, creating
     a heritage fit for your progeny.

You began the unfolding of cosmos,
     before was no being, no void;
World without end was in you and from you,
     yours on that First Day.
     All other gods came after.

The Leiden Hymns

XC

The Nine Great Gods were drawn from your person,
        and in each you shadowed your features;
But it was you shone first
           when you fashioned the world long ago,
      O unseen God
             who hides Himself from all others.

Ancient of ancients,
        elder even than they,
        earth god who fashioned Himself into Ptah,
The very parts of whose body are primeval gods;
      who rose as the Sun amid chaos
To betoken rebirth
        and the rhythms of resurrection;
Sowed the seed of the cosmos as Atum, the Old One,
        from whose godhead were moisture and air,
           Shu and Tefnut, the primordial couple.

He ascended in splendor His throne
           as His heart had determined,
      by His power, alone, overruled all existence,
United Himself and kingship forever
        to remain, to the end of days, sole Lord.

But in the Beginning, Light!
        Light was His first incarnation;
      and the incipient world lay hushed
           waiting in awe of Him;

And He cried the glad cry of the Great Cackler
            over the nomes of His new creation
                        while He was still alone.

He loosened speech:
                  words flowed in the chambers of silence;
        He opened each eye
               that it might behold and be gladdened.
Sounds of the voiceless world began with Him:
        the victory shout of unparalleled God
               shattered silence and circled the world.
He nurtured to birth all things
        that He might offer them life,
    and he taught men to know the Way,
              the path they each must go.
Hearts come alive when they see Him,
     for He is our Procreator, the Power
        who peopled the dark with His children.

The Leiden Hymns

C

When Being began back in days of the genesis,
>> it was Amun appeared first of all,
>>> unknown His mode of inflowing;
There was no god became before Him,
>> nor was other god with Him there
>>> when He uttered himself into visible form;
There was no mother to Him, that she might have born him His name,
>> there was no father to father the one
>>> who first spoke the words, "I Am!"
Who fashioned the seed of Him all on his own,
>> sacred first cause, whose birth lay in mystery,
>>> who crafted and carved His own beauty —
He is God the Creator, self-created, the Holy;
>> all other gods came after;
>>> with Himself He began the world.

The Leiden Hymns

CC

Dark be the changes, and dazzling the incarnations
        of God, God of wonders, of the two firmaments,
           God of the myriad visible forms.
All gods boast they share in His nature —
               but to heighten themselves,
        borrowing splendor on splendor
           from the terrible power of His godhead.

Rê himself joins to shine in God's visible form,
        and God is that Craftsman praised in the City of Sun;
What is said of the earth god in truth pictures Him;
        and when Amun emerged from out the ur-waters,
           it was God's image strode over them.
He flowed forth again as the Eight of Hermopolis,
        procreated the primal deities, was midwife to Rê,
Perfected Himself in Atum — one flesh together;
        and He alone, Lord of all things at creation.

His soul, they say, is that One above,
        and He is the one in halls of the underworld,
           foremost of those in the eastern dwelling;
His soul rests in heaven, His earthly form in the West,
        and His image in Thebes — for worship
           when He shows Himself among men.

But, one alone is the hidden God,
        being behind these appearances,
      veiled even from gods,
        His nature cannot be known;

The Leiden Hymns, from Stanza CC

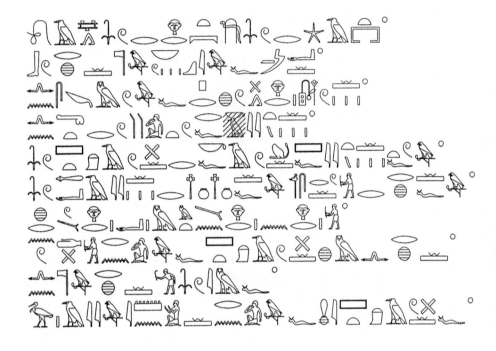

He is more distant far than heaven,
        deeper profound than the world below,
            not all gods in concert discern His true features.
No likeness of Him is sketched on papyri,
        no eye-witness tellings to picture Him.

God is loath to release His full glory,
        great beyond questioning, potent beyond all belief:
Dead on the instant in pain is that unfortunate god
        who utters — even in innocence — God's hidden Name.
No god draws forth godhead by this means;
        God is final, ineffable Spirit,
            past knowing His Name and His mystery.

The Leiden Hymns

CCC

God is three of all gods,
> Amun, Rê, Ptah — these are preeminent:

Past knowing His nature as Amun, the hidden,
> He is Rê in His features, in body is Ptah.

Their cities on earth endure to eternity,
> Thebes, Heliopolis, Memphis, forever;

Word from heaven is heard in the City of Sun,
> told in Ptah's temple to the Handsome of Face,

Who shapes it in signs for Thoth's books of wisdom;
> thus Amun's city records the gods' histories.

For God's judgment is rendered from Thebes:
> when decision emerges, it comes through the Ennead;

Since each move of His lips is most secret,
> gods carry out what He commands.

God's Word, it can kill or perpetuate,
> life or death for all men unfolds by means of it;

And He opens His countenance as Rê, Ptah, or Amun,
> a trinity of unchanging forms.

The Leiden Hymns

D

Defeated and doomed the rebels, down on their faces,
       none now dare to attack Him;
Land freshens once more over erstwhile opponents,
       the dissatisfied cannot be found.

Rampant lion with knife-edged claws, in a swallow
       He drinks the power and blood of pretenders;
Bull, strong-backed and steady, whose hooves
       bear down on foe's neck while horns do their work;
Bird of prey who swoops to seize His assailant,
       talons keen to shred flesh and crack bone!

How He delights to do battle, secure in His puissant arm!
       Hills quake to His tread when the war-fit masters Him,
Earth shakes as He bellows His war-cry,
       creation cowers in fear.
O, woe to any who challenge Him,
       who taste the play of His twin-tipped weapon,
For He, our God, is skilled above any,
       Lord of the deadly horns.

The Leiden Hymns

DC

The mind of God is perfect knowing,
                His lips its flawless expression,
       all that exists is His spirit,
             by His tongue named into being;
He strides, and hollows under His feet become Nile-heads —
          Hapy wells from the hidden grotto into His footprints.
His soul is all space,
             His heart the lifegiving moisture,
       He is Falcon of Twin Horizons,
           sky god skimming heaven,
His right eye the day,
            while His left is the night,
       and He guides human seeing down every way.
His body is Nun, the swirling original waters;
               within it the Nile
      shaping, bringing to birth,
            fostering all creation;
His burning breath is the breeze,
         gift offered every nostril,
      from Him too the destiny fallen to each;
His consort the fertile field,
          He shoots His seed into her,
     and new vegetation, and grain,
        grow strong as His children.
Fruitful One, Eldest,
         He fathered gods in those first days,
     whose faces turn to Him
           daily and everywhere.
That countenance still shines on mankind and deities,
         and it mirrors the sum of the world.

The Nature of the Beyond
The Prayers of Pahery

PAHERY LIVED during earlier Dynasty XVIII and was mayor of el-Kab and Esna. The walls of his tomb at el-Kab offer the most extensive characterization of the Afterlife that survives from ancient Egypt outside the spells of the Book of the Dead. From his prayers and descriptions we can see the function of his tomb and the necessity of regular offerings to sustain his soul. We also follow his vision of what life with Osiris would be like and of the possibilities for moving back and forth between this world (as an invisible spirit) and the next (as one of the glorious redeemed). It is also interesting to note the presence in Pahery's prayers of the concept of "the god within" the living human breast.

The Prayers of Pahery

I. Prayer to the Gods for Offerings

An offering which the king makes: — to Amun,
    Lord of the Thrones of the Two Lands,
King of eternity, Lord of Forever,
    divine Ruler, Lord of the high double plume,
Sole one beforetimes, greatest of Ancients of primeval days,
    without equal, creator of men and gods,
Living flame which rose out of chaos
    in order to lighten the Sunfolk;
And to Nekhbet, the Shining One,
    Mistress of Heaven, Lady of the Two Lands;
To Osiris, Foremost of Westerners,
    Lord of This, great in Abydos;
To Hathor, Mistress of Desert Borders,
    fearless among the gods;
To Ptah-Sokar, Lord of Shetyt;
    to Anubis, Lord of Rosetau;
And to the Enneads, the Greater and Lesser: —

May They give a thousand of bread, beer, meat, and fowl,
    a thousand offerings of provisions,
A thousand offerings of every plant
    which flourishes upon earth,
And a thousand of everything good and pure
    which is offered in the presence of the All-Lord.
And may They receive the bread and drink which is before the Lord of
                                  Eternity
    and the milk which appears upon the offering table,
And the water which gushes forth from Elephantine,
    and the northwind which [blows over the land] —
At the festivals of the Month, the Sixth Day, the Half-Month,
    the Great Procession, the Rising of Sothis,

The feast of jubilation, of Thoth,
    of the First Birth of Osiris, of Isis,
The Procession of Min, the Procession of the Fourth Day,
    the Evening Offering, the Rising of the River,
And the festivals of heaven according to their days
    and according to the daily rituals.

May They provide for you a sacred robe of finest linen
    from those taken from the limbs of the god;
May They anoint you with sacred oil,
    may you drink the water that is left upon the altar,
And may you receive offerings from what is upon it,
    as one honored among the foremost of the blessed.

For the Soul of the Mayor of el-Kab, the scribe Pahery, vindicated,
    filled with devotion to his Lord.

II. Prayer for Life in the Afterworld

May you come and go, while living,
    with joyful heart by favor of the Lord of gods,
With a fine burial in old age,
    after your length of years has come.
May you take your place in your sarcophagus,
    unite with earth in the Western Land,
Become transformed to a living Spirit
    —powerful over bread, and water, and air—
Which may take shape as phoenix or as swallow,
    as falcon or as heron, just as you wish.

May you ferry across without hindrance
    and sail upon the waters of the flood.
May your life return once more—
    your spirit never deserting your body again!
May your spirit be holy among the transfigured,
    and may the blessed hold converse with you;

From The Prayers of Pahery, II

Your likeness is there among them in heaven
        while you are receiving your offerings on earth.

May you have power over water, breathe air,
        drink whatever your heart desires;
May you be given your eyes to see with,
        your ears for hearing whatever is said,
Your mouth for speaking,
        and your feet to walk.
May your arms move for you, and your shoulders,
        your flesh be firm, your muscles thriving;
May you have joy of all your members
        and count your body whole and well.

No evil is accountable to you,
        your heart is with you truly;
Your mind is yours as formerly
        as you go forth to the sky.

May you explore the Afterworld
        in whatsoever shape you shall desire.
May they call you every day
        to the Table of Osiris, who was truly good;
And may you enjoy the offerings in his presence
        and the gifts for the Lord of the Sacred Land.

For the Soul of the Mayor of el-Kab, the Mayor of Esna,
        Counter of Grain from Denderah to el-Kab,
The vigilant administrator, free of wrongdoing,
        the scribe Pahery, vindicated.

III. Prayer Describing the Afterlife

May you eat the loaves in the presence of God
        by the Great Staircase of the Lord of the Ennead;

May you turn from there to the place where He is
    in the midst of the high tribunal of judges;
May you move about freely among them,
    a friend to the Followers of Horus.

May you come and go unhindered
    and not be turned back from the doors of the Otherworld;
May the gates of heaven be opened to you,
    and the very doorbolts unlock of themselves;
May you enter the Hall of Two Truths
    and the god who is in it honor you.

May you be at ease in the underworld,
    travel freely about in the City of Hapy;
May your heart have joy in your ploughing
    in your plot in the Field of Reeds;
May your portion attain what has been set for you
    and the harvest arrive full of grain;
May the draw-rope be taut in the ferryboat —
    Sail to your heart's desire!

May you go forth from the tomb each dawn
    and find your way back each evening.
May they kindle a taper for you at night
    until the sun shines on your breast.
Let them say to you, "Welcome, welcome
    to your house of the ever-living!"

May you gaze upon Rê in the circuit of Heaven
    and glimpse Amun when he shines;
May you be mindful of beauty each day,
    may all that impedes you be driven to earth;
May you spend eternity in gladness of heart
    esteemed by the god who is within you.

—Your heart is with you, it will never abandon you;
    and your provisions endure in their place.

For the soul of the scribe, Pahery, vindicated.

IV. Pahery's Autobiography: His Claim of Rectitude

He says:
I was a nobleman, effective for his lord,
    wise, not negligent.
I proceeded on the path which I sought out
    and came to understand the goal of living.
I reckoned up the farthest limits in those writings
    which dealt with actions of the king;
And all the affairs of the royal palace
    were smooth as Hapy flowing to the Great Green Sea.

My voice was skilled in furthering the interests of my lord,
    concerned as I was with balancing accounts;
I was not neglectful of the payments,
    nor did I profit from the surpluses.
My own heart guided me
    along the path to praises of the king.

My pen made me famous;
    it made my voice heard among the magistrates,
And it enhanced my reputation
    so that I outdistanced noblemen.
[. . . . .] me in the Presence,
    and my good character elevated me—
Summoned as one unbiased and placed in the balance,
    I emerged as one esteemed and trusted, without taint.

I came and went
    with my heart my sole companion.

I did not speak falsely to another person,
 knowing the god who dwells in humankind—
I could perceive Him
 and thus distinguish one path from another.
I acted exactly as commanded,
 did not confuse report with its reporter;
I did not speak the language of the streets
 nor consort with those of little character.

I was one who attained benevolence,
 one praised who came forth favored from the womb.
The Mayor of el-Kab, Pahery,
 begotten of the Prince's tutor, the Scribe Itef-reri, vindicated,
  and born to the Mistress of the Estate, Kam, vindicated.

V. Appeal to the Living

He says:
Pray listen, all you who have now come to be,
 let me speak to you without equivocation.
O living ones, you who exist,
 nobles and commons who are upon the earth,
Servants of God hallowed in their calling,
 each scribe who bears the staff of office,
The one conversant with God's language,
 each one skilled in dealing with subordinates,
  the speaker distinguished for his readings of the liturgy—
May you all give praise to Rê, Lord of Eternity,
 and to Nekhbet, the shining goddess of el-Kab.
And all of you passersby, effective in your varied offices,
 may you live to endow your children!

Just so, may you recite the offering prayer
 in the manner found in the writings

And the invocation offering as spoken by those long dead
    just as it came from the mouth of God.
Anyone who shall here bend his arm
    shall grow in the counsels of righteousness;
To act properly according to tradition
    is to bear witness before this gravestone:
Your thousand of bread, your thousand of beer,
    your hundred-thousand of everything good, true, and pure,
For the osiris, Mayor of el-Kab, Mayor of Esna,
    treasurer on the southward voyage,
        the scribe excellent at reckoning, Pahery, vindicated.

Let me speak to you all,
    help you to understand:
This is a recitation without excesses or exaggerations —
    there is no slander, no disputation in it,
There is no contending with another person,
    no troubling some poor man in his misery.

These are sweet words of consolation!
    The mind cannot be surfeited with hearing them!
The breath of the mouth can never be used up —
    there is no breathlessness, no weariness in this.
Goodness is yours when you perform it
    for [you] discover [that it earns] you favor.

While I was on earth among the living,
    no injustices toward God were counted against me,
        and I became a blessed spirit.
O! I have furnished my house in the realm under God,
    and my share is by me in everything.
Yet I shall not fail to answer a prayer —
    a dead man is father to any who aid him;
He does not forget one who pours water to honor him.
    It is good for you to consider this.

Harpers' Songs

HARPERS' SONGS are a strange survival from ancient Egypt. They seem to fly in the face of all religious tradition; for they express the *carpe diem* theme, "seize the day." As the following two poems clearly state, the end of life brings not a happy afterlife but the grave. Thus, one must enjoy life while one can. The piece from Intef's tomb was copied onto a papyrus in antiquity along with a group of New Kingdom love songs, while that from Inherkhawy's tomb (Dynasty XX, ca. 1160 B.C.) is one of the finest expressions of this theme.

From the Tomb of King Intef
Pap. Harris 500

Song in the tomb of King Intef, vindicated,
in front of the singer with the harp:

He is prospering, this fine prince;
death is a happy ending.

i

One generation passes, another stays behind—
    such has it been since the men of ancient times.
The gods of long ago rest in their pyramids,
    and the great and blessed likewise lie buried in their tombs.
Yet those who built great mansions, their places are no more.
    What has become of them all?

I have heard the words of Imhotep, and Hordjedef, too,
    retold time and again in their narrations.
Where are their dwellings now?
    Their walls are down,
Their places gone,
    like something that has never been.

There is no return for them
    to explain their present state of being,
To say how it is with them,
    to gentle our hearts
        until we hasten to the place where they have gone.

ii

So, let your heart be strong,
    let these things fade from your thoughts.

Look to yourself,
     and follow your heart's desire while you live!

Put myrrh on your head,
     be clothed in fine linen,
Anoint yourself with the god's own perfumes,
     heap up your happiness,
          and let not your heart become weary.

Follow your heart's desire and what you find good;
     act on your own behalf while on earth!
And let not your heart be troubled —
     that day of mourning for you must come;
And Osiris, the Weary-Hearted, will not hear our wailing,
     weeping does not save the heart from the grave.

So spend your days joyfully
     and do not be weary with living!
No man takes his things with him,
     and none who go can come back again.

The Harper's Song for Inherkhawy

A Song Sung by his Harpist for the Osiris,
Chief of the Crew in the Place of Truth,
Inherkhawy, who says:

I am this man, this worthy one,
who lives redeemed by abundance of good
tendered by God indeed.

i

All who come into being as flesh
        pass on, and have since God walked the earth;
               and young blood mounts to their places.

The busy fluttering souls and bright transfigured spirits
        who people the world below
               and those who shine in the stars with Orion,
They built their mansions, they built their tombs—
        and all men rest in the grave.

So set your home well in the sacred land
        that your good name last because of it;
Care for your works in the realm under God
        that your seat in the West be splendid.

The waters flow north, the wind blows south,
        and each man goes to his hour.

ii

So, seize the day! Hold holiday!
        Be unwearied, unceasing, alive,
               you and your own true love;

Let not your heart be troubled during your sojourn on earth,
        but seize the day as it passes!

Put incense and sweet oil upon you,
        garlanded flowers at your breast,
While the lady alive in your heart forever
        delights, as she sits beside you.

Grieve not your heart, whatever comes;
        let sweet music play before you;
Recall not the evil, loathsome to God,
        but have joy, joy, joy, and pleasure!

O upright man, man just and true,
        patient and kind, content with your lot,
           rejoicing, not speaking evil: —
Let your heart be drunk on the gift of Day
        until that day comes when you anchor.

From *The Eloquent Peasant*

THIS TEXT dating to the Middle Kingdom purports to depict events occurring during the reign of King Khety III Nebkaure of Dynasty X (ca. 2050 B.C.). A humble farmer and trader is robbed of his goods by a bureaucrat. He appeals his case to Rensi, the pharaoh's Lord High Steward; and because the eloquence of this humble man is so astounding, Rensi informs the king, who has the peasant detained until he has made nine such appeals. His family is secretly provided for during this period, and all his passionate oratory is carefully written down for the king. At the end, the peasant is rewarded and the petty bureaucrat punished. The theme of the peasant's nine speeches is *ma'at,* one of the most fundamental concepts of ancient Egyptian civilization, representing a union of our terms, truth, justice, and harmony. Here the term is translated as "justice." The peasant's speeches offer one of the earliest treatments ever of that concept.

The Peasant's Eighth Complaint

O Lord High Steward, my lord,
        we fall through curséd greed.
The greedy man, he comes to no good end —
        his seeming triumphs are but moral failure.
You too are greedy, it does not become you;
        you take, there is no benefit to you.

Oh, leave a man alone to seek his own true fortune!
        You have your own belongings in your house,
            your belly's full,
The barley springs so high it bends toward earth,
        its excess dropping to the ground to die.

The one who stops a thief aids the officials.
        Do whatever shall oppose injustice.
The refuge of the hard-pressed man, it is those same officials.
        Do whatever shall oppose deceit.

Fear of your high position hinders my appeal to you,
        yet you cannot know my thoughts —
And so, your quiet man is back,
        and he would make his grievance clear to you.
He should not fear the one to whom he puts his plea,
        nor should his fellow find you absent from the streets.

Your fields lie all about the countryside,
        your grain grows on your grounds,
Your foodstuffs fill the storehouse,
        officials offer gifts to you —
And still you pillage!
        Are you really such a robber?

Is it true whole gangs are dragged along with you
    to confiscate those fields?

Do Justice for the Lord of Justice,
    who is the wise perfection of his Justice.
Reed pen, papyrus, and palette of Thoth all dread to write injustice:
    when good is truly good, that good is priceless—
But Justice is forever,
    and down to the very grave it goes with one who does it.
His burial conceals that man within the ground,
    yet his good name shall never perish from the earth;
The memory of him becomes a precious thing,
    he is a standard written in the Word of God.
Is he a scales? It does not tilt.
    Is he a balance beam? It does not dip awry.

Now, either I shall come, or surely someone else will come,
    and may you condescend an answer!
Do not detain your quiet man for questioning;
    do not attack one who did not injure you.
—You are not merciful, you do not care,
    and yet you cannot flee, you are not able to destroy;
And you certainly can never compensate me for these splendid words
    which pour forth from the mouth of God Himself!

Speak Justice! Do Justice!
    for it is powerful, it is far-reaching, it endures.
All that devotion to it shall discover
    leads on to honor and to veneration.
Does the balance tilt indeed?
    It is still the scale-pan does the weighing.
There never can be excess of high standards,
    nor should a mean act reach the humblest habitation
      until we mingle with the earth.

From *The Maxims of Ptahhotep*

T HIS INSTRUCTION was presumably composed during Dynasty V of the Old Kingdom, since Ptahhotep
served as vizier under King Izezi (ca. 2380–2342 B.C.). The Maxims are one of
the most celebrated of such collections of wisdom, which are comprised of the
experience garnered by a father, usually from a successful public career, and
handed down to a son. Such texts constituted the "philosophy" of all ancient
Near Eastern cultures. The preeminence of such wisdom texts in the Egyptian tradition is seen in the fact that only they tend to have authors' names
attached to them, the remainder of the literature now being virtually anonymous. Such authors were regarded as the sages of the civilization. The Maxims
are exemplified here by the author's opening comments on the travails of old
age and by the first Maxim.

The Maxims of Ptahhotep

Prologue

The Teaching of the Mayor of the Royal City and Vizier, Ptahhotep, under the
Majesty of the King of Upper and Lower Egypt, Izezi, who lives forever and ever.
The Mayor of the Royal City and Vizier, Ptahhotep, says:

> "My sovereign Lord,
> Old age has come, the years weigh heavily,
>   misery my lot, and infant helplessness returns.
> Repose for such a one is sleeplessness each day;
>   the eyes are dim, the ears benumbed,
> Strength ebbs from the faltering heart,
>   the mouth is still and cannot speak,
> The mind is gone and cannot picture yesterday,
>   bones ache from head to toe,
> The nose is clogged and cannot breathe the air,
>   it makes no difference if you stand or sit.
> Good turns to ill,
>   experience has passed you by:
> What old age does to all mankind
>   is heartbreak every way.

> "May you appoint your servant one to lean on in old age;
>   then shall I pass to him words of the judges,
> The wisdom of our forebears,
>   those in the past who listened to the gods.
> Then shall the like be done for you
>   that the troubles of the people be defeated
>   and the Two Banks work for you."

Then the Majesty of this god said:
"Yes, teach him according to the speech of old;
         then he shall be a pattern for offspring of the great,
So that understanding shall sink in by means of him,
         each heart a witness to what he has said.

                    No one is born wise."

Maxim 1

Do not be arrogant because of your knowledge;
        approach the unlettered as well as the wise.
The summit of artistry cannot be reached,
        nor does craftsman ever attain pure mastery.
More hidden than gems is chiseled expression
      yet found among slave girls grinding the grain.

The Maxims of Ptahhotep, I.

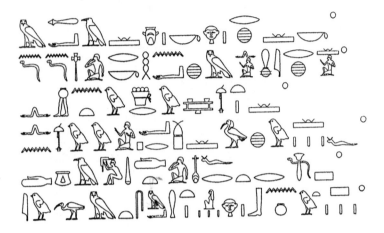

The Instruction for Merikarê

THIS EARLY instruction is attributed to a Heracleo-
politan king of Dynasty X (twenty-first century B.C.)
whose name probably was Khety, though only the *y* remains to identify him.
It was directed to his royal son, Merikarê. The father is a warrior king and has
fought in many battles and has survived dissention, disloyalty, and insurrection
at home. The time is the end of the First Intermediate Period and just before
the Theban dynasts united the country and established the Middle Kingdom.
Here we have a battle-hardened father offering the fruits of his experience
in attempting to bring order to Egypt and form a stable government for the
"citizens" who are loyal to him. He must balance the need to ruthlessly put
down attempted coups with the benevolence and generosity required for civil
order and peace. All his advice—some of it very fine—went for naught; for
not too long after this, the Heracleopolitans lost the civil war with Thebes.

The Instruction for Merikarê

Beginning of the Instruction
Composed by the King of Upper and Lower Egypt, [Khety,]
for his Royal Son, Merikarê

i. Treatment of Insurrectionists

[The first lines are too fragmentary to translate.]

. . . .

Do not tolerate malfeasance;
    arrest the one defying you. . . .

. . . .

    . . . .

If you find a man who is without family —
    a man the citizens do not know —
Whose followers are many in the crowd,
    who serve him for his wealth, ...
Who sidles into hearts, struts before his underlings
    to sow disorder — that man is a traitor!
Destroy him! Kill his children!
    Obliterate his name! Wipe out his associates!
        Erase the memory of him and those who serve him!
Such an agitator will confuse the citizens —
    and he can turn his followers into troops.

If you discover such a one belonging to the citizens —
    whose treason has been hidden until now —
Expose him in the presence of your courtiers:
    Destroy him! he is a rebel,
        a mischief in the City!

Gather the multitude and drive the hothead at it!
    No one faults a man who will destroy a traitor—
        a rogue who takes to arms against his father!

It is the man of humble station who can lead authorities astray—
    and you must end whatever trouble he provokes.
Should the crowd turn ugly, take him into custody;
    but be merciful with him in any punishment you mete,
        and you will turn his terror into joy.

Let your voice be just on the side of God;
    then shall the citizens approve of your devices
        as you move against those who would oppose you.
The heaven of a man is his good nature;
    but the slanders of an angry man are shameful.

ii. The Power of Words

Be skilled in words that you may be strong—
    the king's tongue is his mighty arm;
Words are more powerful than any fighting,
    and none encircle the resourceful man.
The ignorant sit on their mats,
    but wisdom is the bulwark of a leader;
Those who know his knowledge do not test him,
    nor do mishaps happen during his time.
Truth comes to him distilled
    like counsels spoken by the sages of old times.
Do better than your fathers and your forefathers;
    work for a like success through learning.
See how their words endure in the Writings!
    Unroll them, read them, and surpass the wise!
        Each sage was once a wide-eyed pupil.

iii. Advice for Governing

Shun evil; benevolence is comely.
    Make your works endure by means of your supporters;
        prosper the herdsmen connected to the City.
Worship God with offerings and gifts,
    which will enhance your name, testifying to your goodness.
        And pray that you be healthy in your time.

Value your high officials, protect your people;
    strengthen your borders and your border outposts.
        Acting for the future—that is good!
Respect the living man who is sharp-sighted;
    it is the naive man who shall be miserable;
        and let them value you because of your good nature.

Pitiful is he who binds himself to earth while living;
    he is a fool, greedy for what belongs to others.
Life passes by on earth—it is not long—
    and it is good to think upon the mischance in it.
Not one in a million is true to the Lord God of Egypt
    that he might earn the life forever.
Man—made by Him who made Justice—moves on,
    even the devoutest is lost, disappears.

Advance your high officials so that they uphold your laws;
    no partiality exists in one whose house is wealthy.
The man of substance, he will not be narrow-minded,
    but the poor man cannot speak his truth.
Who says, "If only!" cannot be straight-forward,
    for he is partial toward the one he loves—
        he tilts toward the holder of his compensation.

Great is the great One whose great ones are great!
    The king must be an able man, leader of many followers,
        and wealthy too, rich in his high officials.
You must speak truth within your household
    so that officials all across the realm respect you.
Uprightness is the token of a royal lord—
    the foremost house must earn respect from those who serve it.

Be just that you may prosper upon earth:
    soothe the weeper, do not oppress the widow;
Do not deprive a man of his father's goods
    nor interfere with high officials in their functions.
Beware of punishing unfairly,
    and cause no injury—that will not help you!

Discipline by beating or incarceration;
    the land can be secure by this means.
—Except for the traitor whose conspiracy has been laid bare,
    and God knows who is disaffected!
God cuts that mischief down in blood!
    —Yet it is gentleness which lengthens life.

iv. Eternal Life

Do not destroy a man whose godliness you know,
    with whom you used to scan the sacred Writings.
Read what is set down there concerning God
    that your step be firm in the realm of the Mysteries.
The soul goes on to the place it knows;
    it cannot wander back upon its paths of yesteryear;
No sort of supernatural power can keep it
    from reaching Those who give it water.

The Conclave of the gods that judges suffering Man—
    you know They are not lenient

On that day of judging the poor wretch,
  in that hour of weighing out his life.
    And it is painful when the guilty is a wise man.
Do not fill your heart with length of years,
  for They see lifetimes as an hour.

A man lives on after his final mooring,
  and his deeds are heaped beside him.
Existence over There is certainly forever,
  and one who takes it lightly is a fool;
But one who reaches there free of wrongdoing—
  he shall live on like a god,
    wide-striding like the Lords of all eternity.

v. Further Practical Advice

Raise up fresh troops so that the Residence will favor you;
  increase your servants by employing veterans.
See how your people are renewed out of the coming generation—
  and this for twenty years now!—
Young troops eager to pursue their calling,
  veterans marching forth from the reserves,
The raw recruit turning himself into a soldier,
  sharpened by his training.
—It was old comrades who fought for us
  when I recruited them at my accession.

Honor your high officials, advance your trusted men,
  give gifts freely to the young troops in your retinue;
Equip with knowledge, furnish fields,
  provide with cattle.
Do not prefer the rich man's son over the humble—
  you should pick a man according to his deeds.
Further all crafts and skills
  in keeping with the wishes of the Lord of Power.

Guard your border and build your fortresses
    so that troops can be effective for their Lord.
Fashion your many monuments to God —
    it makes the name live on for him erecting them.
And a man should also do what benefits his soul:
    acting as priest at the monthly service,
        wearing the white sandals,
Enriching the temples,
    hallowing the Mysteries,
Attending in the holy sanctuary,
    and breaking bread in the House of God.

Freshen God's offering tables, increase the loaves,
    provide additional attendants —
It benefits the one who does this —
    and maintain your monuments in keeping with your wealth.
A single day contributes to eternity,
    an hour embellishes the future.
        Through service to Him, one is known to God.
Your fame shall travel to far distant lands —
    so far they cannot accurately describe them.

vi. Conduct toward the South

It is madness to lay waste an enemy's possessions;
    yet the enemy must not take ease within the Royal City!
Troops will be fighting troops
    just as our ancestors foretold:
"Egypt shall fight in the graveyard
    hacking up tombs in a frenzy of destruction."
I did this, and thus it happened:
    God acted as toward anyone who sins this way.

Do not be at odds with the noble Southern Region —
    you know the palace prophecy concerning it.

And it has happened with this very outcome:
>they cannot be invaded, just as had been said.
I turned on Thinis opposite its southern border at the Valley;
>and I overran it like a cloudburst—
>>not even blesséd Meryibrê ever did this thing!

Be considerate in governing because of this;
>move slowly therefore, reinvigorate the ties.
No amount of scrubbing can wash away this deed.
>Good means acting for the future.

It will be good for you to ally with the South
>which comes as a neighbor bringing gifts;
I acted just as our blesséd forebears had—
>if its grain failed, I supplied it.
Be gracious since they are the weaker party—
>protect yourself by sharing your bread and beer.

Granite comes to you without impediment,
>so do not mar another's monuments!
You can hew stone in the Tura quarries,
>so do not build your tomb by demolition—
>>those are a villain's deeds!

See, a king *can* have happiness!
>Your eye may rest when you sleep because of your strength;
You may do what you will because of what I have done:
>there are no enemies within the circuit of your borders!

vii. Pacification of the North

An upright man arose, Lord of the City,
>whose heart was dismayed by the Northland
From House of the Tree over to Sembaq City
>with its southern border at the Two Fish Canal.

I pacified the western part entirely
      as far as the sand dunes of the Lake Country—
They cultivate it now in order to grow cedar-wood,
      and juniper trees are planted to supply us.
The eastern hills are infested with the bowmen-nomads,
      so their revenues are negligible.
The central Delta has been recovered, and all those in it;
      the towns strengthened, so that they respect me.

The land which was laid waste is now developed into nomes
      and the numbers of its citizens increased;
The rule of one lord now is in the hands of ten men,
      the official is given revenues reckoned from the taxes,
The freeman is provided with a farm—
      and he will labor for you like a gang of workmen!
        No disaffection will appear among them.

Hapy cannot trouble you by not appearing,
      so the revenues of Lower Egypt are in your keeping.
Now the line against the Asiatics has been drawn—
      the one I fashioned in the East—
From the boundaries of Hebenu to Horus' Way,
      settled with citizens, filled with Egyptians,
From among the choicest of the land
      to build an opposition to them.
I need a brave man to pursue this,
      to go beyond what I have done.
        But have a care: too much zeal spawns evil progeny!

And this you can say of the barbarians:
      the accursed Asiatic, life is dreadful where he lives—
Lacking water, unfriendly due to the many trees,
      the paths difficult because of the mountains!
He will not stay in one place,
      going off because of want, wandering the hills on foot.

He has been fighting since the time of Horus:
  he cannot conquer, nor can he be conquered!
Nor will he indicate the day of battle,
  like a thief who skirts the fringes of the camp.

But as I live and hope to live,
  these barbarians were actually within the boundary wall—
Fortresses were breached and garrisons imprisoned—
  and I had Lower Egypt cut them down!
I carried off their households and retainers,
  I seized their cattle,
I killed Egyptians who were on their side,
  until the Asiatic hated Egypt.
Do not trouble your heart about him:
  he is an Asiatic, a crocodile upon a sandbank;
He may control a lonely pathway,
  but he will not attack a town of many people.

Medenyt is reunited with its district,
  its one side under irrigation to the Bitter Lakes.
It is a knife against the bowmen:
  its walls are strong, its warriors many,
The workers in it know how to handle weapons—
  not to mention the freemen who are there.
The district of Memphis totals ten thousand men,
  as well as commoners and untaxed freemen;
Officials have been in it since it was the capital;
  its borders are secure and its fortresses are strong.
Countless Northerners irrigate it for me over toward the Delta,
  cultivating grain beside the freemen.

It would be surpassing me for one who could accomplish it—
    look, it is the gateway to the Delta!
And they have excavated a canal to Neny-nysw—
  its citizens are many, and are loyal.

But beware of sorties by allies of the enemy:
    caution prolongs one's years!

Your border toward the south of it is in confusion —
    it is the nomad-bowmen who don the war-kilt there.
Build centers in the Delta;
    a man has no small name through his accomplishments!
A city well-established cannot be destroyed —
    so build, build temples for your royal statues!
        The enemy, he only loves intrigue and evil chances.

viii. Royal Conduct

As the late King Khety maintained in his teaching:
    "Be silent toward the brazen man who slights the offerings;
        God will settle with this enemy of His.
What he has done will turn upon him,
    and he will catch himself in his own trap!
Such a one cannot beg sympathy
    on that awful coming day.
        Enrich the offerings and worship God!"

Do not say, "The will is weak!" Do not slack your efforts!
    And act to curb your anger — which injures heaven.
Content is worth a hundred years of monuments! —
    and even if the enemy knew, he could not disturb it.
Do not admire the one who colors his accomplishments —
    there is another who comes after him!
        And there is no lack of enemies!

He must be One who knows, the Lord of the Two Banks;
    the king, head of his entourage, must not act foolishly;
He must be wise upon his coming from the womb,
    for God distinguishes him — one before millions of men.

It is a magnificent responsibility, the kingship:
 it has no son, it has no brother.
What makes your works endure?
 It is one man ennobling another.
A man should act toward one who was before him
 so that what he had accomplished is enhanced
 by that other who comes after him.

Now, an awful thing happened in my day:
 the nome of Thinis was destroyed!
It happened, though no deed of mine,
 for I learned of it after it was done.
Yet see the monumental evil I had caused:
 to destroy is villainous indeed!
No benefit accrues to one who would restore what he has wasted,
 ruin what he has built, embellish what he has defaced.
Oh, guard yourself against it:
 one pays blow for blow —
 and everything there is becomes oppression!

ix. Meditation on God the Creator

The generations come and go among mankind,
 and God, who knows all natures, still lies hidden.
None lifts a hand against the powerful,
 and everywhere the eye sees ruin;
One worships whatever god is met upon the way,
 made of enduring stone or born from metal.
And yet the thirsty reservoirs are filled with waters of the flood,
 nor is there river yet that can conceal Him,
And it is He who frees the stopped canal,
 for in such ways His veiled Spirit moves.

The gone soul journeys on to whence it came,
 nor can it ever stray to paths of yesteryear.

So "make your home fine in the West," they said,
        "raise high your seat in the realm under God" —
But through care in accomplishing Justice!
        The hearts of the very gods lean on Justice.
Esteemed are the gestures of the upright heart
        more than the gift-ox of one who does wrong.
Act so toward God that He acts thus toward you.
        But rich provisions, they only green altars;
What conduct carves, thence your good name.
        And God well knows who serves Him.

Provide for mankind, the flock of God,
        for He made earth and heaven for their sake;
He soothed the raging darkness of primeval waters,
        and He created heart's breath that they might have life.
They are His living images, come from His very self,
        that He might shine forth in the heavens upon them.
And He created for them plants and foliage,
        and small beasts, fowl, and fishes were their food.
Yet He destroyed His enemies, diminished His own children,
        when they, ungrateful, planned revolt against Him.

For their sake He created light
        that He might sail about the sky to see them;
He wove a holy dwelling round about them:
        and when they weep, He hears.
He created for them godly rulers from the womb,
        leaders to fortify the backbones of the weak;
He gave them supernatural power to be a weapon
        and to counteract the blows of fate.

Watch over them, by night as well as day.
        God has struck down the rebel hearts among them
Much as a father disciplines his son to ease his brother.
        And God knows every name.

From The *Instruction for Merikarê*, ix, from stanza 3

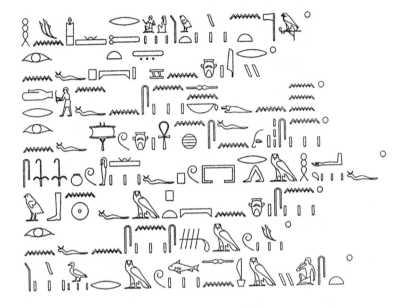

x. Conclusion

You must not harbor any ill against me
    who offer all the precepts for a king.
Pay heed to them that you may live to be a man!
    Then you shall equal me, and none complaining.

Do not destroy one who would be near you—
    God, who knows him, is recommending him to you!
It is such a one will one day rule on earth;
    and they are also gods who are retainers of the king.
Offer your love to all—
    that signifies good character, as the years pass.
And it shall be said of you, "He who ended the time of calamity,"
    by those who come after in the House of King Khety

    —with our prayers for its ending today!

Now I have told you the things effective for me.
    Act in accordance with what has been set before you.

The Wisdom of Amenemopet

The *Wisdom of Amenemopet* is the culmination of surviving texts in the genre of the didactic or hortatory pieces usually called instructions. Amenemopet's words strike the reader as offering some of the most mature, apt, and vivid observations on the conduct of life to survive from ancient Egypt. Many can still be read with profit. The situation is the usual one in wisdom texts—a father distilling the advice gained over a lifetime of public service and formulating it to pass it on to his son. Amenemopet is a high official dealing with the agricultural affairs of the government, while his son, Hor-em-maa-kheru, is a trained scribe in the service of the god Min. Beyond the statements concerning public conduct and behavior, there are broader, more general observations on the conduct and meaning of life which deepen and enrich these maxims.

The Wisdom of Amenemopet

Prologue

Beginning of the meditations on good living,
    the guide to health and happiness,
The various regulations for gaining entrée to officials,
    and the customs of the courtiers;
To know how to reply to one who speaks to you,
    to bring back a report to one who sends you;
To help you enter upon the Way of Life,
    to keep you safely while on earth,
To help your mind withdraw into its chapel—
    which can provide an oar to steer through evil;
To rescue you from the mouths of the crowd,
    one praised in the speech of good people.

Composed by the Minister of Agriculture, wise in office,
    scribe of the seed-corn of Ta-Mery,
Overseer of grain, regulator of the corn-measure,
    who gathers in the harvest for his lord,
Who registers the islands which are come forth newly
    according to the Royal Titulary of his Majesty,
        and places markers at the borders of the fields;
Who exempts the king's name from the tax lists,
    creates the land-register for Egypt,
Institutes the offerings to the gods,
    and grants holdings to the poor;
Overseer of grain, administrator of provisions,
    who supplies the silos with their stores;
A thoughtful man, just in Abydos of the Thinite nome,
    vindicated in Achmim;

Owning a pyramid in the precinct of the West
   and a chapel in Abydos—
Amenemopet, son of Kanakht,
   vindicated in This.

This for his son, the youngest of his offspring,
   smallest of his associates,
Keeper of the Secrets of Min-Kamutef,
   who dispenses the holy water of Osiris,
Who installs Horus on his father's throne,
   protects him in his splendid shrine,
Guards the sacred mysteries for his Lord,
   observes the omens for the mother of the god,
Tends the black cattle of the Terrace of Min,
   and protects Min in his shrine—
His name: Hor-em-maa-kheru,
   child of a high official of Achmim,
And son of a musician for Shu and Tefnut,
   Taweseret, chief chantress in the Horus Temple.

I

Give ear to hear my words,
   and give your mind to searching into them.
Great benefit is yours if you will place them in your heart,
   while failure follows the neglect of them.
Let them rest within the strongbox of your body,
   let them provide a lock upon your heart—
Sea-lost is he who is a storm of words—
   let these provide an anchor for your tongue.
If you will live your life with all this in your heart,
   you shall find in it the means to be successful;
You will find my words a treasure-house for living,
   and you yourself shall prosper upon earth.

II

Avoid demeaning the already miserable
    by any show of strength against the weak.
Do not raise your hand against the aging
    nor criticize the conversations of the great.
Do not formulate your messages in an abrasive manner
    nor envy one who does.
Do not raise a cry against the man who injures you,
    and do not you yourself reply.
One who does evil—the deep canal will get him;
    and its moving waters, they will bear him off!
The Northwind, it descends, darkening his hour,
    dragging him into the howling storm;
The clouds pile high, the crocodiles are restless,
    and this fevered man of yours—how does he fare?
It is his voice up there crying before the Highest,
    and the Moon above shall specify his crimes.
"Ply the oars that the evil one may cross to Us,
    We have not seen his like before."
—Raise him up, give him your hand,
    hurl him into the arms of God;
Fill him with bread at your table
    so that he be satisfied and be ashamed.
This too is a thing dear to the heart of God—
    let a Man go slow before speaking.

III

Do not start a quarrel with the hot-mouthed man
    nor be disdainful toward him in your speech;
Be deliberate before an adversary, bow to a foe,
    and sleep on what you think before you speak.
A stormwind moving like a flame in straw—
    that is the hot-head in his hour!

Yield before him, leave the bellicose man
    to the god who knows how to mend him.
If you spend your days with these things in your heart,
    your offspring shall live to see them.

IV

A man of the temple who is intemperate
    is like a tree which grows indoors.
In a short moment its leaves and blossoming are finished
    so that its journey ends on the rubbish heap;
It floats to its final destination
    and its burial is fire.
But the truly thoughtful man, though he keeps himself aside,
    is like a tree growing in sunlight;
It greens and flourishes, it doubles its harvest,
    standing before the face of its Lord;
Its fruit is sweet, its shade is pleasant,
    and it ends its days in the garden.

V

Do not hold back the portions meant for the temple —
    do not be greedy as the way to wealth;
Do not defraud God's servant
    merely to profit someone else.
And do not say, "Alas, today is like tomorrow!"
    —How can you arrive at this?
Come tomorrow, today is in the past —
    look, floodwaters brim the well-mouths,
The crocodiles are loose, hippos rest in the shadows,
    the fish are leaping,
Small beasts are filled, birds are ecstatic,
    full nets are drawn ashore.

And all the thoughtful men of the temple
    say, "Great is the gift of Rê!"
Consider the thoughtful man that you may discover Life,
    and you yourself will flourish upon earth.

VI

A

Do not move the markers at the edges of the fields
    nor alter findings of the measuring-cord;
Do not be greedy in distributing the holdings
    nor violate the boundaries of the widow.
The furrows of the plough are cultivated for a lifetime—
    and the swindler covets them;
But should he get them, lyingly and falsely,
    surely he will fall at last to the Moon's justice.
Keep watch on one who does this while on earth—
    he is a despoiler of defenseless people,
He is a foe, wreaking havoc on your very body,
    and malice dwells in his eye.
His household is declared a public enemy
    and his granaries are leveled to the ground;
They seize his goods out of his children's hands,
    and the little that he had is given to another.

B

Avoid unsettling the boundaries of the fields
    that the fear which you inspire may be ended;
One pleases God through the Moon, his viceroy—
    and it is he who sets the limits of the cultivation.
Take care to keep your own self healthy,
    and be circumspect before the Lord of All.
Do not obliterate the furrow of another;
    to have his good opinion strengthens you.

Plough your own fields to find your own sufficiency,
    receiving what is made on your own threshing floor.
Better one bushel which God gives
    than five thousand got by fraud.
—No one spends time now growing provisions,
    no one commands that the vessels be filled,
Hardly at all do they work in the granary—
    day breaks and they all are gone.
More splendid the poor in the hand of God
    than an overflowing storehouse;
More splendid the loaf, with heart's content,
    than riches full of care.

VII

Let not your heart lust after riches—
    one can never ignore fate or fortune.
Let not your thoughts take you too far—
    each man is a man of his time.
Be not concerned with seeking increase—
    sufficient to you are your own possessions.
If riches come through misappropriation,
    they shall never stay the night under your roof;
Come daybreak, and they are not with you,
    one seeks their dwelling but they are not there;
The ground yawns open and they enter, swallowed,
    sunk below into the netherworld.
They make themselves a hollow fit to hold them
    and settle into their dark prison,
Though they would fashion wings like ro-geese
    and fly upward to the heavens.
Do not let dishonest riches please you,
    yet do not yearn for poverty—
If the bowman is ordered forwards,
    his hand must be steady and sure.

The sea-ship of the greedy sticks on the mud-flats
 while the skiff of the thoughtful man slips free.
Pray to the Aton rising,
 saying, "Give me content and health!"
He will provide what is needful for living
 and let you be free from dread.

VIII

Let your integrity be felt in the vitals of the people,
 so that each and every one may look to you.
Praise the holy Serpent,
 spit upon Apophis;
Let your tongue be free of words which injure
 so that you inspire devotion in the masses.
Thus shall you take your seat within God's house
 and present your offerings to your Lord;
You shall reach blessedness, find rest within your grave,
 and prosper in the everlasting majesty of God.
Do not cry out "Criminal!" against a man—
 the circumstances of his flight may be unknown.
If you hear a good man saying something evil,
 leave it outside the place where it was heard;
Have the good report ready on your tongue,
 let the evil be concealed within your body.

IX

Do not be friends with the intemperate man
 nor let him draw you into conversation.
Keep your tongue from talking back to your superior,
 and do not curse him;
For he may frame his words so as to trap you
 or dismiss you for your insolence.
Seek advice on answering from a man of your own station
 and avoid offending him.

Pass by the speeches of the always aggravated man
     faster than wind over wave —
He is one who destroys, builds only with his tongue,
     so that he speaks of things in empty words.
He answers, aching to do battle,
     and his purpose is to injure;
He fosters strife among all people,
     loading his speech with lies.
He knits a slippery meaning out of intertwisted words,
     fighting and quarreling he comes and goes,
Then dines at home
     while his retorts are festering outside.
One day his wrongs will rise to censure him,
     woe to his children then!
If only Khnum would take him back into his hands —
     to the potter's wheel with the hot-mouthed man! —
That He might knead some sense into his senseless skull.
     For he is like the jackal's offspring in the cattle-pen:
It turns its eye against its own companions,
     it makes the herdsmen gibber,
It runs before the wind like stormy weather,
     it dims the brightness of the sun,
It flicks its tail like the young crocodile,
     it leaps upon its prey —
Its lips are sweetened, its tongue darts out,
     and a fire burns in its belly.
Make no attempt to humor such a one —
     let the respect that once you offered be no more.

X

Do not antagonize the angry man with provocations —
     you only trouble your own heart;
And do not praise him with false praise
     though fear is in you.

Do not speak untruths among the people —
      that is abhorrent to God;
Do not divide your thinking from your tongue
      in order that your schemes might be successful.
Be grave and serious before the many —
      and let the outcome lie with God.
God hates lying speech,
      and he detests the man with a sour belly.

XI

Do not covet the little that the poor man has
      nor hunger for his bread;
The poor man's mite sticks in the craw,
      it is a theft that catches in the throat.
Should a man gain his purpose through perjury and lying,
      his heart will rot in his body;
For enmity weakens accomplishment,
      and guilt is unproductive of good.
Should you stand guilt-laden before your superior,
      you will be unsuccessful, whatever you say —
Your flatteries will be countered with curses
      and your kissing the earth with a beating.
Stuffing your mouth with food — gorging and vomiting —
      cuts you off from your better self.
Watch carefully the supervisors of the poor man —
      staves beat him,
His people are confined in hobbles,
      and his workers hounded to the place of execution.
Should you be lax before your own superior,
      you will be censured by subordinates.
See that you act as steering-oar for the poor man on his journey,
      watch over him and be respectful of his goods.

XII

Do not be greedy for a great man's goods
  when your mouth is filled with food abundantly and freely;
Should he appoint you to administer his holdings,
  his wealth will be an enemy to your well-being.
Do not bandy words with an intemperate man
  nor let the malcontent be close to you.
If you are sent to ferry chaff,
  its very bulk is hateful;
But if one fears to carry a demeaning message,
  he will never be sent out again.

XIII

Do not deceive, in writing or accounting—
  that is a hatefulness to God.
Do not testify with perjured words
  nor undercut another with your tongue;
Do not give hard reckoning to one with little,
  and do not let your pen be harsh.
If you discover a great arrears borne by a humble man,
  divide it into three,
Throw away two and let the one remain—
  thus it will be like walking on the path of Life,
And you will spend your nights in sleep until the morrow,
  and find it satisfies like good advice.
More splendid the praise from the heart of the people
  than an overflowing storehouse;
More splendid the loaf, with heart's content,
  than riches full of care.

XIV

Do not curry favor with any man
  nor trouble to seek out his hand;

If someone says, "I beg you, take these gifts!
    There are no needy people here to see it."
—Do not glance at him, do not nod your head,
    do not demean yourself by your reaction.
Say words if you must, tell him your admiration,
    so he will cease to bother you.
Yet do not totally disdain him at his first arrival
    lest at another time he might return.

XV

Do good in order to attain a richer life;
    never dip the reed-pen to do wrong;
The beak of the Ibis is the finger of the scribe—
    take care that you are worthy of it.
The Baboon sits in his temple at Hermopolis,
    and his eye roves over Egypt;
He watches for the one with cheating finger,
    and he sweeps that man's subsistence into the flood.
As for the scribe who falsifies his writing,
    his son will not be entered in the scribal annals;
But if you spend your days with these things in your heart,
    your children shall see them happen.

XVI

Do not displace the balance-beam, nor falsify the weights,
    nor alter the proportions of the measure.
Do not be greedy for the produce of the fields
    nor misuse goods belonging to the treasury.
The Baboon sits beside the balance
    and his heart is hidden—
O, what god is like great Thoth,
    the Creator who devised these things for us!
Do not make weights to cheat by,
    they are certain to bring down God's wrath;

If you see another cheating,
	make a wide path around him.
Do not be greedy for copper,
	despise fine linen;
What are they for, the linen skirt and the clothing?
	this is pretense in the presence of God!
All this transmuting what glitters into gold—
	day dawns and it is still straw.

XVII

Do not falsify the grain measure
	or tamper with its parts.
Do not withhold the overflow belonging to the laborer
	since his is the empty belly;
Measure out as if it were the portion for a friend—
	your hand thus reaches out toward righteousness.
Do not construct a bushel that makes you double portions;
	rather, act in keeping with the height of this year's flood.
The bushel-measure is the Eye of Rê,
	and it hates the one who robs;
The measurer who gives excess dishonestly—
	the anger of His Eye is over him.
Do not expropriate the harvests of the tiller
	nor set it down in writing to defraud him.
Do not conspire with the measurer of grain
	nor interfere with workers in his employ.
Great in its power is the granary threshing-floor—
	greater than an oath by the Great Throne.

XVIII

Do not lie abed fearing tomorrow;
	day breaks, what will it be?
		Man cannot know what the morrow will bring.

The Wisdom of Amenemopet, XVIII, lines 1–7

God dwells amid His perfections,
    man must live with his failure;
And the words which men speak are fleeting,
    and the creatures of God pass away.
So, say nothing that gives injury,
    do not you yourself cause pain—
Even though harms attributed to God
    be sealed with His own finger.
As there is no perfection apart from God's hand,
    so nothing flawed lives in His presence;
And should He wish to be rid of perfection,
    He can destroy it all in an instant.
Be serious of heart, steady your thoughts,
    and do not use your tongue to steer by.
Or say man's tongue is the rudder of a ship,
    the Lord of All is still pilot.

XIX

Do not be careless in court in the magistrate's presence,
    do not falsify your words
Nor ramble in your answers—
    your testimony must hold firm.
Do not hesitate because of the oath to your own lord—
    speak out in the hall of interrogation;
Tell the truth before the magistrate
    lest he pass sentence on you yourself.
If at a later date you enter his presence,
    make him lean on your every word
So that he will repeat what you say to the Thirty in chambers
    and use it time and again.

XX

Do not mislead the members of the Council,
    and do not undermine the Truth.

Do not be swayed by fashionable clothing
    nor turn away from those in disrepair.
Receive no favors from the powerful
    nor hound the weak man for the great man's sake.
Truth bears the greatness of God,
    He gives it freely through His love;
And the might of one who champions Truth
    ends suffering by destroying it.
Do not enact dishonest laws —
    they defile the legacy of the dead,
They are a great forswearing of sworn duty,
    they are like the garbled speeches of a messenger.
Do not blacken someone's character upon papyrus,
    do not intervene in God's affairs,
And do not take upon yourself the wrath of God —
    it can never bring good outcome or good fortune.
Award the world's goods to their rightful owners,
    and for yourself seek Life;
Do not build your mind amid their dwellings —
    though your bones be destined for the place of slaughter.

XXI

Never say, "I have found a powerful overlord;
    I can abduct any man from your city."
Nor say, "I have found an eminent protector;
    I can hurt the one I hate."
For truly, you do not know the mind of God,
    nor can you perceive the morrow;
Seat yourself in His arms
    that your peace may be anchored within them.
The crocodile, he roars his invitation out of the waters
    but respect for him is slight —
Do not empty out your belly to the world
    nor act to lessen its esteem for you;

Do not let your words circle among the crowd
      nor make yourself familiar with the chatterer.
More effective is the man whose accusation stays within him
      than the one who tells it to his own confusion.
One does not rush about to reach perfection
      nor create a thing in order to destroy it.

XXII

Do not provoke a companion who is agitated
      nor prevent him speaking out the matter on his mind,
Do not fly up to put him in his place —
      you cannot know what he is thinking.
Be aware beforehand of his views,
      and be calm and soothing to attain your goal.
Put the matter to his face that he may empty out his belly,
      understand the nature of what he has disclosed;
Point his feet aright, and do not shame him,
      respect him, do not turn away.
For truly, you do not know the mind of God,
      nor can you perceive the morrow;
Seat yourself in His arms
      that your peace may be anchored within them.

XXIII

Do not break bread in the presence of a nobleman
      nor fill your mouth ahead of him.
If you would satisfy yourself, pretend to chew —
      take pleasure in your own saliva,
Look at the drink in front of you,
      and let it suffice for your necessities.
The great official in his magnanimity
      is like the multitude of wellsprings in the Delta.

XXIV

Do not eavesdrop on proceedings of a judge in chambers
     nor repeat them to anyone outside;
And do not have your own opinions broadcast
     so that your ideas are not compromised.
The mind of Man is the breath of God—
     beware lest He turn His back.
And the man in conversation with a high official,
     make no attempt to overhear his name.

XXV

Do not laugh at a blind man, do not joke at the deformed,
     do not contribute to the misery of a cripple,
And do not mock a man who is in God's hands
     or taunt him when he goes astray.
Man is clay and straw,
     God is the potter.
He tears down and He builds up every day,
     creating small things by the thousands through His love;
And He creates men by the thousands too as overseers
     while each is in his hour of life.
What joy it is for the creature who reaches the West—
     he is safe in the presence of God.

XXVI

Do not sit about the tavern
     waiting to attach yourself to some distinguished person
Whether he be newly in his office
     or a man of years with children.
Content yourself with those of your own station
     and Rê will help you prosper from afar.
If you should see a great man in the street,
     follow along behind him out of respect;

Lend a hand to an old man gone on beer,
    and honor him as his own children would.
A strong arm is not weakened by discretion,
    nor is one's back made safe by bowing.
They do not let a man who speaks kind words be poorer
    than the mighty man whose words are straw;
And the Pilot who watches from afar —
    He will not let His ship capsize.

XXVII

Do not defame a man more eminent than you —
    he knew Rê before you;
Do not complain to Aton when he rises
    saying, "It is someone else maligns the great."
That is bad form indeed in the august presence of Rê,
    a small man cursing his betters.
Say that he beats you — your hand stays at your side!
    Say he berates you — you remain silent!
If on the morrow you enter his presence,
    he will gladly give you provisions.
Remember, the dependant is dog of his master,
    he barks for the one who feeds him.

XXVIII

Do not misuse a widow if you find her in the fields
    nor fail to set aside your work to speak with her;
Do not let a stranger pass your beer jug thirsty,
    refill it time and time again before your friends —
Give love to the god of the ruined and poor
    far exceeding your debt to the eminent.

XXIX

Leave no one behind for the River crossing
    as you maneuver to launch the ferry.
If an oar is assigned you in the midst of the flood,
    stretch out your arms to grasp it;
As none are abhorrent to the hand of God,
    so no distinction is made among rowers.
Do not on your own take the ferry out
    nor be over-concerned with collecting fares;
Take the fare from the hand of the one who has it
    and pass by the one without.

XXX

Mind carefully these thirty chapters—
    they delight, they instruct;
They are the best of books;
    they help the ignorant to know.
If they are read out in the hearing of the untaught man,
    he will come to treasure what they say.
Peruse them, store them in your heart,
    help the young interpret them
        as they study with their teachers.
The scribe who is proficient in his calling
        shall rise to be a trusted Friend at court.

Epilogue: The Immortality of Writers

Those writers known from the old days,
    the times just after the gods —
Those who foretold what would happen (and did),
    whose names endure for eternity —
They disappeared when they finished their lives,
    and all their kindred were forgotten.

They did not build pyramids in bronze
    with gravestones of iron from heaven;
They did not think to leave a patrimony made of children
    who would give their names distinction.
Rather, they formed a progeny by means of writings
    and in the books of wisdom which they left.
The papyrus roll became their lector-priest,
    the writing-board their loving son;
Books of wisdom were their pyramids,
    the reed-pen was their child, smoothed stone their spouse.
In this way great and small became inheritors;
    and the writer was the father of them all!

What they built of gates and chapels now are fallen,
    their soul-priests and their gardeners are gone,
Their headstones undiscovered in the dirt,
    their very graves forgotten.
But their fame lives on in their papyrus rolls
    composed while they were still alive;
And the memory of those who write such books shall last
    to the end of time and for eternity.

Be a writer! Set your heart upon it
    so your name shall be like theirs!
A book is finer than a graven stele,
    more than a memorial wall.
Those men built pyramids and chapels of the mind
    to make their names renowned!
Surely it is a thing of glory, in the land beyond,
    that one's name be fresh in the speech of mankind.

Man dies, his body is dust,
    his family all brought low to the earth;
But writing shall make him remembered,
    alive in the mouths of any who read.
Better a book than a builded mansion,
    better than body's home in the West,
Splendid above a fine house in the country
    or stone-carved deeds in the precinct of God.

Are there any here today like Hordjedef?
    Is there another like Imhotep?
There has not come in our time one like Neferty
    or Khety, the best of them all.
I give you the names of Ptahemdjehuty
    or Khakheperreseneb.
Is there another like Ptahhotep
    or the equal of Kaires?

Those sages who saw into the future —
    what came from their mouths came to be;
It is found as wisdom and truth
    inscribed on their papyrus rolls.
The children of others are given to them
    to be co-heirs with their own;

And the sacred knowledge they saved for the world
    can be followed and known in their writings.
They themselves are dead and gone,
    but their names are immortal in books.

Colophon

This was its outcome

from beginning to end

as found in writing.

CHRONOLOGY

Thinite Period	Dynasties I–II	ca. 3007–2682 B.C.
Old Kingdom	Dynasty III	ca. 2682–2614 B.C.
	Dynasty IV	ca. 2614–2479 B.C.
	Dynasty V	ca. 2479–2322 B.C.
	Dynasty VI	ca. 2322–2191 B.C.
	Dynasties VII–VIII	ca. 2191–2145 B.C.
First Intermediate Period	Dynasties IX–first half XI	ca. 2145–2020 B.C.
Middle Kingdom	Dynasty XI, second half	ca. 2020–1976 B.C.
	Dynasty XII	ca. 1976–1793 B.C.
	Dynasty XIII	ca. 1793–1645 B.C.
Second Intermediate Period	Dynasties XIV–XVII	ca. 1645–1550 B.C.
New Kingdom	Dynasty XVIII	ca. 1550–1292 B.C.
	Dynasties XIX–XX (Ramesside Period)	ca. 1292–1070 B.C.
Third Intermediate Period	Dynasties XXI–XXV	ca. 1070–655 B.C.

| Late Period | Dynasties XXVI–XXXI | ca. 655–332 B.C. |

Late Period   Dynasties XXVI–XXXI   ca. 655–332 B.C.

Ptolemaic Period   ca. 332–30 B.C.

Roman Province   ca. 30 B.C.–A.D. 330

Source: After J. von Beckerath, *Handbuch Der Ägyptische Königsnamen* (Mainz am Rhein: von Zabern, 1999.)

GLOSSARY

Abu. The town of Elephantine in the far south of Egypt proper, near the present-day city of Aswan. Source of stone for monuments and the collecting point for ivory from the south.

Abydos. Very ancient Egyptian city north of Thebes, seat of the kings of Dynasties O, I, and II (the Thinite Period) and prime religious center of Egypt; home of the worship of Osiris.

Achmim. City some hundred miles north of Luxor; center for the worship of Min.

Admonitions. A subcategory of instructional or didactic literature ("wisdom texts") warning against moral and social evils.

Adversary, The. See Apophis.

Akhenaten, King. Monotheist king of later Dynasty XVIII. Reigned 1351–1334 B.C. He worshipped a single god, the Aten, denying the existence, or at least the worship, of the other gods, and initiating profound changes in Egyptian religion and art. His religion did not outlast him.

Amenemhat I, King. First king of Dynasty XII, toward the beginning of the Middle Kingdom. Reigned 1976–1947 B.C.

Amenemopet. Author of *The Wisdom of Amenemopet,* probably from Dynasty XX. Perhaps the finest of the moral instruction texts to survive from ancient Egypt. Written in verse lines in the original.

Ameny. Shortened form for King Amenemhat I. See entry above.

Amun. The Hidden One, King of the Gods. An ancient god who rose to prominence at Thebes during Dynasty XI and the Middle Kingdom to become the great cosmic, imperial, and universal god of New Kingdom Egypt.

Amunenshi. Ruler of Upper Retenu in twentieth-century B.C. Syria-Palestine. Appears in *The Tale of Sinuhe.*

Amun-Rê. Fuller name of Amun (see prior entry) as that god absorbs the power and functions of Rê, the earlier sun and creator god of Heliopolis.

Andjety. Ancient god worshipped in the Delta and precursor of Osiris, into whose nature he blends.

Anglo-Saxon. Also called Old English (A.D. 450–1100).

Ani. Owner of one of the finest and fullest copies of *The Book of the Dead*. Lived at the end of Dynasty XVIII.

Antagonist, The. See Apophis.

Anubis. God of the dead, of embalming, and of the necropolis. The prime funerary god before the rise of Osiris.

Apophis. Cosmic serpent-demon who attacked the sun god's (Rê's) barque each night, thus endangering the cosmic order. Defeated each night, he was reborn each day. One of the fixed elements in the universe, symbolizing chaos; hence, the Great Antagonist or the Adversary of the sun god.

Asheru. The sacred lake and divine precinct about the Temple of Mut at Karnak in ancient Thebes.

Asiatics. Peoples to the northeast of Egypt in Syria-Palestine and Mesopotamia (the Fertile Crescent in general).

Aten (Aton). Sun god symbolized by the disc of the sun. Becomes the sole god during the reign of Akhenaten in the fourteenth century B.C.

Atum. The Old One (the Totality) and Lord of the Ennead. An early version of the sun god and creator of the universe. The center of his worship lay at Heliopolis. Succeeded in his functions by Rê, also of Heliopolis.

Atum-Horakhty. Atum as he was identified and fused with Horus of the Two Horizons, the figure of the rising sun of the new day. In this conception, Rê himself was the sun as seen during the major part of the day and Atum was the old, or setting, sun.

Ba. An aspect of the personality, according to the ancient Egyptians. Continuing after death and often described or depicted in the form of a bird. The closest approximation (but not an exact equivalent) is our word "soul."

Baboon. Animal sacred to Thoth and often a name for the god.

Barque of Rê. The ship in which the sun god travels at night to move through the darkness from the west to the east to begin the new day.

Bastet. The feline goddess of Bubastis.

Battle of Kadesh. Battle fought by Ramesses II in his fifth regnal year (1275 B.C.) against the Hittites at the town of Qadesh (Kadesh) on the Orontes River in Syria-Palestine. It was, in effect, a defeat for the Egyptian forces; but the personal valor of the king was celebrated in a kind of mini-epic poem, *The Battle of Kadesh,* which survives in many copies, both on papyri and on monuments.

Bee. Emblem of Lower Egypt. See "He of the Sedge and the Bee."

Beginning, The. Egyptian term for the moment or time of creation, "The First Occasion." The account takes various forms but describes the emergence of order from chaos. The primary account has the creator god appearing on a primal hill that emerges from the midst of the primeval waters and on which he stands to accomplish the work of creation.

Belles-lettres. "Literature" as works of art (for ancient Egypt, consisting primarily of tales and myths, various types of instructional or didactic material ["wisdom texts"], complaints and laments, hymns, prayers, and love songs). Not "literature" in the broader sense of anything written down.

Bitter Lakes. Area of the northeastern Delta?

Black Land. A common name for Egypt, referring to the black of the fertile soil as opposed to the "red" of the sterile desert.

Book of Kemyt. Text from Dynasty XI or XII, later used as a schoolboy text during the New Kingdom. A compendium of useful vocabulary, forms, and usages for the aspiring scribe.

Busiris. Ancient city in the central Delta. In religious traditions the home of Osiris. The name derives from *Pr Wsir,* "the House of Osiris."

Byblos. Very ancient city on the eastern Mediterranean coast, located in what is now Lebanon. There was Egyptian contact with Byblos from the earliest dynasties.

Cartouche. The oval within which were written the fourth and fifth names (the pre-nomen and nomen) in the royal titulary.

Champollion, Jean François (1790–1832). Decipherer of Egyptian hieroglyphic writing in 1822.

Chaos. The condition of things before creation of the universe by the sun god. Conceived of as a turmoil of water, wind, and darkness. Chaos continues outside the formed universe, and beings like Apophis try to force a return to the original state of disorder.

Chaucer, Geoffrey (ca. 1343–1400). Most famous poet writing in Middle English.

Children, The. The royal offspring of both sexes, at least in *The Tale of Sinuhe.*

City of Sun. Ancient Heliopolis, center of worship of the sun god.

Coffin Texts. Religious texts consisting mainly of spells to aid the deceased. Carved or painted on the coffins of nobles from Dynasty XI to XVII, they had a wider range of themes and subject matter than the Pyramid Texts, which were limited to kings and queens.

Coming Forth. Literally, the ability of the deceased's spirit to emerge from the tomb after death to enjoy the benefits of this world. A kind of resurrection—especially for Sinuhe after his reception by the king following the living death of his lifetime exile.

Coptic. The final phase of the ancient Egyptian language (from the third century A.D. on), written in the Greek alphabet with additional characters derived from the hieroglyphs. The only stage of the Egyptian language to write out the vowels. Coptic was gradually replaced by Arabic after the Arab Conquest in A.D. 640.

Craftsman, The. Epithet for the god Ptah in his function as inventor of crafts and protector of artisans.

Creator God. The first god and the one who created the universe from chaos. In various versions of the myth and over the long span of Egyptian history, he was the cosmic Horus, Atum, Rê, Ptah, Amun, Aton, or Amun-Rê.

David, King. Israelite king of the United Monarchy. Reigned ca. 1000–961 B.C.

Day Barque. The skyship used by Rê while crossing the heavens during the day.

Death the Crocodile. Personification of the moment of death as being seized and devoured by crocodiles lurking in the Nile. An unpleasant way to die.

Deir el-Medineh. Village of craftsmen and artists who decorated the rock-cut royal tombs in the Valley of the Kings during the New Kingdom. Finds from a trash-pit there have resulted in thousands of ostraca, many with portions of the classic literature of ancient Egypt.

Delta. The northern portion of Egypt (north of modern Cairo) where the Nile River fans out to empty into the Mediterranean Sea. Also called Lower Egypt.

Demotic. A very cursive form of the hieratic writing of the ancient Egyptian language. Used in books and documents primarily from Dynasty XXV to the Roman period (ca. 750 B.C. to fourth century A.D.).

Denderah. Egyptian town just north of Thebes. Sacred to Hathor, whose Ptolemaic temple there is one of the best preserved in Egypt.

Diodorus Siculus. Roman historian, flourishing under Caesar and Augustus (ca.60–30 B.C.). Wrote a world history, Book I of which dealt with Egypt.

Djoser (Zoser), King. Ruled during Dynasty III (ca. 2665–2645 B.C.). Owner of the Step Pyramid at Saqqara, the world's first monumental building made of stone.

Dynasty. Term used to designate a coherent succession of Egyptian rulers, usually a "royal house"; that is, several generations of one family succeeding to the throne, son after father. In actuality, the succession was not this neat. Nevertheless, the priest Manetho (see entry below) used this principle to divide the historical span of ancient Egypt into thirty-one such dynasties.

Eastern Horus, The. The cosmic Horus as lord of lands east of Egypt. Possibly Horakhty, "Horus of the Two Horizons," where the sun rose and set.

Eight Great Gods (Ogdoad). The Eight Great Gods personify elements of the chaos preceding creation of the world, according to the traditions of Hermopolis. They existed in male-female pairs and were Nun and Naunet (the primitive watery abyss), Heh and Hehet (infinite space), Kek and Keket (darkness), and Amun and Amaunet (invisibility or hidden power).

Elephantine. City at the south of Egypt, near the present city of Aswan.

Elder Horus, The. The ancient cosmic sky and sun god depicted as a falcon (whose eyes were the sun and the moon) and known from earliest dynastic times. To be distinguished from the child Horus, son of Isis and Osiris.

El-Kab. Town in southern Egypt about halfway between Thebes (Luxor) and Elephantine (Aswan). Home of the tutelary goddess of Upper Egypt, Nekhbet.

Elohist, The. Anonymous Israelite writer who composed the northern version (Ephraimite) of the traditions of Israel. Fl. ca. 850 B.C.

Ennead (Nine Great Gods). The original generations of gods according to the cosmogony of Heliopolis. The creator god, Atum, without consort fathered Shu (air or space) and Tefnut (moisture), whose children were Nut (sky) and Geb (earth). Their offspring were the Osirian family: Osiris, Isis, Nephthys, and Seth. Later, the child Horus (different from the cosmic [or elder] Horus) was added as born to Isis after Osiris' murder by Seth.

Enneads, Two (The Greater and the Lesser). The Greater consists of the nine gods of the Heliopolitan cosmogony while the Lesser stems from Horus, child of Isis and Osiris. When the two are spoken of together, all gods of the Egyptian pantheon are meant.

Esna. City south of modern Luxor. Site of the Ptolemaic Temple of Khnum.

Eye. One of the most potent symbols known to ancient Egypt for its power of destruction and healing. Originally the left eye (the moon) of the god Horus; it was torn out by Seth and restored by Thoth (the *wedjat*-eye), becoming a potent symbol of protection. In another of the myths, the Eye simply leaves in anger and needs to be recovered, its anger being conveyed by its retributive and punishing power. Hathor, for instance, goes down from heaven as the Eye to destroy mankind, which had plotted mischief against Rê.

Eye of Rê. The royal uraeus, a serpent-goddess, sometimes personified by either Hathor or Sakhmet as agents of Rê's judgment or vengeance. Often carries out the punishment of evildoers, as when humankind plotted to rebel against Rê.

Ezekiel (fl. ca. 593–573 B.C.). Biblical prophet during the Exile, when the Children of Israel (actually, of Judah) were conquered by King Nebuchadrezzar of Babylon and deported (ca. 597 B.C.) to the city of Babylon, where they remained until Cyrus of Persia took Babylon in 539 B.C. and allowed the exiles to return to their homeland. These events took place during the twenty-sixth Egyptian Dynasty.

Falcon. Form of the cosmic sky god and royal god, Horus.

Falcon, The. Specifically referring to the king as earthly embodiment of the cosmic Horus while on the throne of Egypt.

Fashioner, The. An epithet for Ptah, the divine artisan and craftsman.

Field of Reeds. Egyptian *Sekhet Iaru.* Along with the *Sekhet Hetepu,* the dwelling of the blessed dead.

First Day. See "Beginning, The."

First Intermediate Period (ca. 2145–2020 B.C.). Encompasses Dynasties VII–XI.

Followers of Horus. The deified rulers of predynastic Hierakonpolis. Sometimes, the blessed dead.

Fort Horusways. Fort on the northeastern border guarding the main road from Egypt to Syria-Palestine.

Geb. Earth god, according to the Heliopolitan cosmogony. Consort of Nut, the sky, and father of Osiris, Isis, Nephthys, and Seth.

Giza. Northern end of the great Memphite necropolis and site of the pyramids of Khufu, Khaefre, and Menkaure (Cheops, Chephren, and Mycerinus) as well as the Sphinx and many mastaba-tombs of Old Kingdom nobility.

God. A deity, or the ultimate deity. Egyptian religion was polytheistic except during the reign of Akhenaten, who was a monotheist. However, in individual hymns and prayers, and profoundly in the Leiden Hymns, the singular ("God") is used as if no other deity exists for the duration of the hymn or prayer. In the Leiden Hymns the theological problem of the many in the One is specifically addressed so as to make the ultimate Godhead apparently monotheistic, with the other gods as incarnations or variant forms of the ultimate deity. Some scholars prefer the term "henotheists" to "monotheists."

Golden Horus. Designation for the third of the five names in the royal titulary.

Golden One, The. Epithet of Hathor, especially in her capacity as goddess of love.

Great Cackler, The. Also "The Shrieker." Form of the creator god (here, Amun) as a goose or falcon that creates the world by laying a great cosmic egg.

Great Goddess, The. Epithet of various goddesses, perhaps in some contexts as a kind of mother-goddess.

Great Green Sea. Usually the Mediterranean Sea, but sometimes apparently the Red Sea (as in *The Tale of the Shipwrecked Sailor*). Probably, its root meaning is "the open sea."

Great Salt Sea. Probably the marshy area of the eastern Delta, where Sinuhe wandered on his way to Syria-Palestine.

Ha. God of the desert regions (and oases) west of the Nile Valley and Delta.

Hall of Two Truths. The place of final judgment of the deceased in the Afterlife, where the heart is weighed in the balance against the feather of Ma'at, or Truth.

Handsome of Face, The. Epithet for Ptah of Memphis.

Hapy. God of the Nile inundation. Not so much a deity of the River itself as of the energy of renewal and fertility that returned each year with the overflowing of the Nile.

Harper's Songs. A kind of funerary poem generally found in tombs, chanted by a harper (often blind) sitting before the deceased owner [or owners] of the tomb. Its theme is the finality of death, and it urges the living to "seize the day," to enjoy life while it lasts, for tomorrow it will be gone. The type seems very un-Egyptian, yet it is found on walls right alongside traditional poems and spells extolling the joys of the Afterlife.

Harpist. One version of the ancient Egyptian lyric poet or performer. He appears not only in the harper's songs but also helps provide music in the company of other musicians, singers, and dancers at banquets of the living.

Hathor. Ancient goddess often represented in the form of a cow. In some myths she is the mother of the king, while her usual function is as either a funerary goddess or the goddess of love, music, and dancing.

Hathors, The Seven. Goddesses of fate acting collectively and determining the destiny of the child at birth.

He of the Sedge and the Bee. Referring to the king, especially to his prenomen (the fourth name of his royal titulary), as the one belonging to the Sedge of Upper Egypt (the Valley) and to the Bee of Lower Egypt (the Delta), thus uniting the Two Lands.

Hebenu. Capital of the sixteenth Upper Egyptian nome.

Hedj-hetep. God of weaving.

Heliopolis. Ancient city northeast (and now a suburb) of Cairo. Center of worship of the sun and creator god, primarily as Rê but also as Atum, Khepri, and Rê-Horakhty. Source of the theology of the Ennead.

Heracleopolis. City just south of the Fayyum. Capital of Dynasties IX–X and setting for a number of classic pieces of Middle Egyptian literature, such as *The Instruction for Merikarê* or *The Eloquent Peasant*.

Hermopolis. City about midway between ancient Memphis and Thebes. Center for the worship of Thoth and source of the theology of the Ogdoad (The Eight Great Gods).

Herodotus. Greek historian who visited Egypt ca.450 B.C. Egypt is treated in Book II of his *Histories*.

Hieratic. The cursive form of the ancient Egyptian language adapted for rapid writing by reed-pen and ink on papyrus, pottery, or stone. It uses the same signs as the hieroglyphs, but much abbreviated.

Hieroglyphic. The original forms of the signs of the ancient Egyptian language in pictorial form. There is a rough analogy to "block-printing" (hieroglyphic) as opposed to "handwriting" (hieratic). Originally used for carving signs into stone by means of a chisel.

Horemmaakheru. Son of Amenemopet, for whom the *Wisdom* is written.

Hordjedef, Prince. Son of King Khufu (2579–2556 B.C.) of Dynasty IV, and one of the sages of ancient Egypt. A fragmentary *Instruction,* or wisdom text, reputedly by him, still exists.

Horus. One of the oldest and most complex gods of the Egyptian pantheon. Originally a sky god in shape of a falcon, he has three primary forms: (1) the cosmic Horus, the sky god; (2) Horus as incarnated in the reigning king of Egypt, the pharaoh; and (3) Horus the child, son of Osiris and Isis. Other forms of Horus seem to be manifestations of these three.

Horus of Foreign Lands. Probably the cosmic Horus as lord and protector of foreign lands.

Horus of Twin Horizons. Horakhty. The cosmic Horus as sun god of the east and west, the two horizons where the sun rises and sets. Seen usually as a separate god, primarily of the sunrise.

Horus, The. First name of the royal titulary, signifying the king as an incarnation of Horus, first as the cosmic deity, but also as the child of, and successor to, his deceased royal predecessor, who at death is assimilated to Osiris.

Horus' Way. Road from Silê in the northeast Delta to southern Palestine.

House of King Khety. The ruling family of Dynasty X.

House of Millions of Years. The tomb.

House of the Tree. Locale in the western Delta.

Hymn. A major genre of ancient Egyptian literature. A poem praising or worshipping a deity, the divine king, or, on occasion, a city (Thebes), or an object (the personified Red or White Crowns of Egypt). Its purpose is homage.

Hypselis. City in Middle Egypt mentioned in *The Great Hymn to Osiris* as a center of his worship.

Iaaw. Father of the god of the western desert, Ha, but otherwise unidentified.

Iawesh. Possibly, a people or a place whose chieftains Sinuhe offers to bring back to his sovereign, King Senusert I.

Ibis. Animal sacred to Thoth and often a name for the god.

Imhotep. Flourished during the reign of King Djoser (2665–2645 B.C.) in Dynasty III. Architect of the Step Pyramid at Saqqara; physician and sage; author of a book of wisdom (not extant). His reputation became so great that he was deified in later dynasties.

Inherkhawy. Owner of Tomb 359 at Deir el-Medineh in western Thebes. He was Chief of Workmen in the Place of Truth (i.e., the necropolis). He lived during the reigns of Ramesses III and IV and was buried ca. 1150 B.C.

Instructions. The prime didactic genre of ancient Egyptian literature. These are usually cast as the wisdom of a father, who has led a public life, being passed on orally as a series of maxims to a son so as to prepare him in turn for government service.

Inundation. The annual overflowing of the Nile, bringing new silt for the farmer's fields and making life in Egypt possible.

Isis. Great mother goddess, daughter of Geb and Nut, sister and wife of Osiris, and mother of Horus. In the Osirian legend, after the murder of her husband by Seth (also their brother), she searches for the pieces of his dismembered body, resurrects him, and bears his posthumously conceived son, Horus, who upon his majority appeals to the great Ennead of gods for his rightful inheritance, the land of Egypt, which request is granted him by the divine tribunal.

Isle of Flame. A locality in the otherworld. Or, also, the original hillock in the midst of the primeval waters on which the sun god came into being.

Itef-Reri. Father of Pahery.

Izezi (Isesi), King. Penultimate king of Dynasty V, reigning ca. 2380–2342 B.C. Served by the famous vizier, Ptahhotep.

Judges. Public officials who "heard" cases and offered judgments from the earliest times. They also acted collectively as the "qenbet," the council of elders, whether at the local, nome, or national level.

Ka. An aspect of the personality as envisioned by the ancient Egyptians. Like the concept of the *Ba,* it has no counterpart today. It represents something like the "vital energy" of the universe, particularly as embodied in a person, and thus implies creative force or the sustainment of life. The deceased is said to "go to his *Ka*" when he dies.

Kaires. One of the authors named as classic by a New Kingdom scribe who gives a list of the most famous wise men of Egypt. Nothing of his survives.

Kam. Mother of Pahery.

Kamutef. Epithet of Amun, "Bull-of-his-Mother," as the god of procreative force and sexual fertility.

Kanakht. Father of Amenemopet.

Keshu. Possibly a location in Syria-Palestine. From *The Tale of Sinuhe.*

Khakheperrêseneb. One of the great classical authors of ancient Egypt, living during the Middle Kingdom. A (fragmentary?) complaint of his survives.

Khentymenutef. A celestial being who takes the deceased king to Geb. Also, an epithet of Horus.

Kheperkarê, King. The prenomen, or fourth name in the royal titulary, of King Senusert I, second king of Dynasty XII. Reigned ca.1956–1910 B.C.

Khepri. A form of the creator sun god, represented in the form of a scarab beetle, imaged especially as the sun god at dawn rising from the eastern horizon and pushing the sun's disk across the sky. In one myth the sun god is Khepri in the morning, Rê at noon, and Atum (the old one) sinking to the western horizon at sunset.

Khety. Duauf's son. Author of Dynasty XII who is credited with writing "Hymn to the Nile," *The Testament of Amenemhat, King of Egypt,* and *The Instruction for Little Pepi (The Satire on the Trades).* He is called by a New Kingdom scribe, "the best of them all." Not to be confused with King Khety of Dynasty X, who wrote *The Instruction for Merikarê.*

Khety III, King. Probable author of *The Instruction for Merikarê,* and predecessor of that king at Heracleopolis during Dynasty X. Reigned during the twenty-first century B.C.

Khnum. God manifested as a ram, a potter god who creates and shapes life on the potter's wheel. He controls the annual inundation of the Nile from its once-presumed source at Elephantine in the south of Egypt.

Khonsu. Moon god, especially prominent at Thebes, where he is considered the child of Mut and Amun, thus completing the holy family of Thebes.

Khor. Syria.

King of Upper and Lower Egypt. Appellation for the king, using his prenomen or fourth name in the royal titulary and emphasizing his dominion over both the Delta and the Nile Valley to the south.

Kush. The foreign land to the south of Egypt; present-day Sudan.

Lady of Red Peak. "Goddess of the Red Mountain," of the Gebel el-Ahmar northeast of Cairo, in the neighborhood of Heliopolis. Site of a quarry operating from the Old Kingdom on.

Lady of the Stars. Possibly, Nut, the sky goddess.

Lady of Waters. Here, Neith, ancient goddess of Sais, with various functions and legends. Mother of Sobek as creator god and the Ennead in "The Hymn to the Nile."

Lake Country. Area of the western Delta near the Mediterranean Sea.

Lake of Death. Symbol for death as occurring in crocodile-infested waters.

Laments. Or "complaints." A subcategory of ancient Egyptian literature, belonging primarily to the didactic genre, in which the author expresses grief and mourns over some state of affairs. Cf. *The Lamentations of Ipuwer* or *The Complaints of Khakheperrêsoneb.*

Land of Papyri. Epithet for Lower Egypt or the Delta.

Land of Sedge. Epithet for Upper Egypt, the Nile Valley.

Lapis lazuli. Mineral of bluish or bluish-green color, not native to ancient Egypt, used as a gemstone.

Late Egyptian. The stage of the Egyptian language comprising the vernacular of Dynasties XVIII–XXIV (ca. 1550–700 B.C.). Used for literary texts during the New Kingdom and later, but usually mixed with forms from the classical Middle Egyptian stage of the language (except in business documents and letters).

Leiden. City in The Netherlands. The rich collection in the museum there includes Pap. Leiden I 350, which contains New Kingdom hymns from the time of Ramesses II called *The Leiden Hymns to Amun and Thebes.*

Letopolis. City in the lower western Delta north of Giza. Referred to in *The Hymn to Osiris* as a cult center for that god.

Libyan Desert. The desert area west of Egypt.

Libyans. The peoples living to the west of Egypt.

Literal translation. A translation that is essentially a word-for-word carryover from one language to another, respecting the word order of the original and using the root or denotative meanings of the original vocabulary. It does not mean to, or attempt to, emphasize the aesthetic values inherent in the original text.

Literary translation. A translation that, building upon an accurate literal translation, attempts to present the original as a work of art. It emphasizes nuances of words, word echoes, patterns of images and comparisons, tone or mood in the work, sound harmonies and dissonances, characterization, setting, poetic form and genre, and all the devices which transform a "text" into a "poem" or other piece of literature.

Lord of Ma'at. Or "Lord of Justice." In *The Eloquent Peasant* the epithet refers to Rê as creator and regulator of the universe. *Ma'at* includes our concepts of justice, truth, goodness, and universal harmony.

Lord of the Two Lands. Epithet of the king of Egypt.

Lord of the Universe. Epithet usually referring to the creator and sun god Rê.

Lords of Truth. The Ennead of gods sitting as a divine tribunal in judgment, here between the claims of Horus and Seth.

Lower Egypt. Northern Egypt above modern Cairo; the Delta.

Luxor. The modern city that partially overlies ancient Thebes on the east bank of the Nile.

Luxor Temple. New Kingdom temple toward the south of modern Luxor, built primarily by Amenhotep III (1388–1350 B.C.), with additions by Tutankhamun (1333–1323 B.C.), and with later major additions by Ramesses II (1279–1213 B.C.).

Ma'at. One of the most fundamental concepts of ancient Egyptian civilization. It is too broad and too extensive a concept to be translated by any one word, but it designates a combination of our concepts of "justice," "truth," "goodness," and "harmony," the last especially in the sense of cosmic harmony or order in the universe. Creation occurred according to its principle; the pharaoh must rule under its auspices; and people must live by its dictates.

Maaty Canal. One of the first localities (somewhere south of Saqqara) mentioned by Sinuhe on his flight into Syria-Palestine.

Manetho. Egyptian priest who lived during the third century B.C. in the Ptolemaic Period. He wrote a now-lost *History of Egypt* and is responsible for organizing the Egyptian kings into dynasties.

Medenyt. Locale in the Fayyum area?

Medjai. People from a land to the south, in Nubia. Also at times a professional term: auxiliary troops, policemen, or hunters.

Memphis. The greatest of ancient Egyptian cities, along with Thebes to the south. It stretched for miles across the River from modern Cairo and was the administrative center for the government. Its two great burial fields are Giza and Saqqara.

Menna. Historical personage from Deir el-Medineh during the Ramesside period and author of a literary letter to his son, Pay-iry.

Meryibrê, King. The first king of Dynasty X at Heracleopolis during the First Intermediate Period (twenty-first century B.C.). Author of a lost instruction cited in *The Instruction for Merikarê.*

Merikarê, King. Ruled during Dynasty X (perhaps mid–twenty-first century B.C.) at Heracleopolis. Recipient of the *Instruction* apparently written by King Khety.

Middle Kingdom. Encompasses Dynasties XI (second half)–XIII (ca. 2020–1645 B.C.).

Mighty Goddess, The. Variant of "The Great Goddess." Possibly, Sakhmet.

Min. God of sexual procreativity, usually represented as ithyphallic.

Min-Kamutef. Min as "Bull-of-His-Mother," emphasizing the reproductive aspect of the god.

Mistress of the Underworld. Isis?

Mistress of Us All. Epithet of the queen.

Montu. War god of the Theban area, prominent in Dynasty XI and gradually replaced by Amun. Called "Lord of Battle" in *Sinuhe.*

Moon. The moon god Thoth.

Most Holy of Places. Name for the Temple of Karnak in Thebes, domain of Amun.

Name. An essential part of a person. To know someone's name is to have power over that person or deity for good or ill.

Necropolis. Literally, "City of the Dead"; the cemetery or burial ground. In ancient Egypt the necropolis was indeed as elaborate as a city, with streets and houselike tombs. It was a flurry of activity, with priests performing the daily rituals at the tombs and with family members arriving to visit the dead, especially on festival days. The most famous of the necropoli were at Giza, Saqqara, and Thebes. See also "Place of Truth."

Neferbau. A deity mentioned in Sinuhe's letter to Senusert I.

Nefertari, Queen. Great Royal Wife of Ramesses II.

Nefertem. God of the lotus. Son of Ptah and Sakhmet.

Neferty. One of the classic authors of ancient Egypt, who lived during Dynasty XII. Author of a "Prophecy" (backdated to the time of King Sneferu of Dynasty IV) that described Egypt as overrun by Asiatics from the east and that prophesied the coming of a savior called Ameny (Amenemhat I) from the South to restore order.

Neferu, Queen. Daughter of Amenemhat I of Dynasty XII (1976–1947 B.C.) and Great Royal Wife of Senusert I (1956–1910 B.C.). Patroness of Sinuhe.

Nekhbet. Vulture goddess of el-Kab. Mistress of the White Crown of Upper Egypt and protectress of the king.

Neny-nysw. Heracleopolis, capital of the Dynasty X rulers.

Nephthys. Youngest goddess of the Osirian generation in the Heliopolitan cosmology, sister of Osiris, Isis, and Seth. Functions mainly as a mourner for the deceased, usually as paired with Isis.

Nepri. The god of grain. He becomes assimilated into the figure of Osiris.

New Kingdom. Encompasses Dynasties XVIII–XX (ca. 1550 B.C.–1070 B.C.).

Night Barque. The skyship used by Rê for his nightly journey through the Afterworld.

Nile River. With its headwaters in Lake Victoria, and with a length of about 3,400 miles, the Nile's water and silt make life possible in Egypt. As Herodotus said, "Egypt is the gift of the Nile."

Nile Valley. Strictly, Upper Egypt. The portion of Egypt where, over the eons, the river has cut into the bedrock of northeastern Africa to form a valley between bluffs or cliffs.

Nine Great Gods. See "Ennead."

Nomen. The last of the five names in the royal titulary, emphasizing the king as "Son of the Sun God, Rê." This is the name by which Egyptian pharaohs are familiarly known.

Nomes. Term for the districts or "counties" into which ancient Egypt was divided. They probably in some manner reflected the original area of prehistoric settlement. There were twenty-two such districts in Upper Egypt and twenty in Lower Egypt, each with its distinctive emblem and cult center.

Northland. The Delta.

North Wind. A cool breeze bringing refreshment to living and dead alike. Since the Nile flows north, the north wind aids the ships sailing south against the current.

Nubians. Peoples to the south of Egypt.

Nun. Designation for the original swirling, windy, and dark watery chaos preceding creation.

Nut. The sky goddess, wife of Geb, the earth.

Ogdoad. See "Eight Great Gods."

Old Egyptian. The earliest known stage of the Egyptian language, dating from Dynasties I–VIII (from about the thirty-first century B.C. to ca. 2145 B.C.). It is the language of the Pyramid Texts and of the inscriptions on Old Kingdom tombs.

Old Kingdom. Encompasses Dynasties III–VIII (ca. 2682–2145 B.C.).

Orion. The constellation seen as a very ancient star god who strides across the sky, and, after disappearing at dawn, is resurrected each night. He can confer status on the newly deceased king (as with Unis) by proclaiming him "one of the Great Ones."

Osiris. One of the greatest gods of ancient Egypt. Son of Geb (earth) and Nut (sky) he represents both the ideal of the good king and the grain, which dies and is reborn. The legend of his marriage to his sister, Isis, his murder by his brother, Seth, the subsequent birth of his son, Horus, and the awarding of the rule of Egypt to Horus by the divine tribunal of the Ennead sitting in judgment between him and Seth—all these form what is perhaps the richest and most complex myth to survive from that culture. He becomes the god of resurrection; and his example demonstrates that one can overcome death and enter into a happy Afterlife.

Ostraca (sing., ostracon). Pieces of smoothed limestone or bits of pottery with writing or drawing on them.

Ounas (Unis), King. Last king of Dynasty V. Reigned 2342–2322 B.C. On the walls of his burial chamber are carved the first version of the earliest major body of religious texts in the world, the Pyramid Texts. They comprise spells, sayings, hymns, and other material designed to aid in the resurrection of the dead king.

Our Great Lady. Perhaps, an epithet of Sakhmet, especially as the one who causes and removes the plague. Possibly a mother goddess.

Our Lady of Love. The goddess Hathor. The term is used primarily in the love songs.

Pahery. Scribe of the Treasury and Mayor of el-Kab and Esna, he lived in mid–Dynasty XVIII (the mid–fifteenth century B.C.). The inscription in his tomb gives the fullest surviving description of what life in the next world was thought to be like.

Papyrus (pl., papyri). "Paper." Strips were cut from the stem of the papyrus plant, flattened, and glued together into sheets. This became the writing surface used throughout ancient Egyptian history.

Pay-iry. Troublesome son in *Menna's Lament*.

Pepi. Son of Khety and the one for whom the *Instruction for Little Pepi* (often called *The Satire on the Trades*) was written.

Pepi, King. There were actually two kings of Dynasty VI with this name, Pepi I (2310–2260 B.C.) and Pepi II (2254–2194 B.C.). Both had Pyramid Texts carved in their tombs.

Peten. Unknown locale in the Great Salt Sea marshes of the eastern Delta.

Philae. Island in the Nile just south of modern Aswan. Site of a major temple of Isis and one of the last places celebrating the ancient religion.

Place of Truth, The. Designation for the necropolis, especially that of western Thebes. All the men of Deir el-Medineh worked in "The Place of Truth."

Pomegranate nome. The district of Middle Egypt in the Fayyum; its major center was Heracleopolis.

Pope, Alexander. British poet (1688–1744).

Pound, Ezra. American expatriate poet (1885–1972).

Pot marks. Scratched or incised markings on the surfaces of pottery (or other material) of the Thinite Period (Dynasties I–II, ca. 3007–2682 B.C.). Most of the signs are undeciphered, but they are sometimes accompanied by royal names.

Prayers. Ancient Egyptian poems similar to the hymns but requesting something of a deity rather than simply offering homage.

Prenomen. The fourth of the five royal names, emphasizing the king's rule over a united Egypt as "He of the Sedge [of Upper Egypt] and the Bee [of Lower Egypt]." Like the nomen, it is enclosed in a cartouche.

Prosody. That aspect of stylistics or poetics which deals specifically with versification, that is, with the rhythms or meters of poems.

Ptah. The creator god of Memphis. Husband to Sakhmet and father of Nefertem. He created the universe by thinking it and speaking out the names of its parts.

Ptahemdjehuty. Mentioned by a New Kingdom scribe as one of the great writers of ancient Egypt. Nothing of his survives.

Ptahhotep. Old Kingdom sage, vizier to King Izezi (2380–2342 B.C.) of Dynasty V, and author of the *Maxims,* the oldest didactic text to survive complete from ancient Egypt.

Ptah-Sokar. Ptah in his particular identification with the Memphite necropolis.

Punt. Country down the Red Sea coast in eastern Africa. Source of tropical goods and exotic merchandise.

Pyramid. At first, the burial place only of pharaohs (and sometimes their immediate family). Seen by the Egyptians as the earthly dwelling of the god-on-earth who has now gone to his true home with the other gods. The royal pyramid tradition continued from late Dynasty III (Djoser) through the Middle Kingdom. There are over forty of them. During the New Kingdom even the nobles would often have a small pyramid of their own attached to their tombs.

Pyramid Texts. The body of religious spells, sayings, hymns, and other material carved into the royal tombs of Unis (Dynasty V) and the kings (and some queens) of Dynasty VI, to aid them in their journey to the next world, the realm of the gods where they properly belong.

Qa-nefer. Name either of the mortuary temple or of the pyramid complex (or "city") of Amenemhat I, Queen Neferu's father.

Qedem. Locale in Syria-Palestine visited by Sinuhe.

Queen of Heaven. Epithet applied to various goddesses, perhaps Nut here. Which one is referred to in the "Song of the Princesses" in *Sinuhe* is not clear.

Quiet Man, The. Designation for the ideal man in the Egyptian instructional or didactic tradition. The concept cannot be translated by a single word. The man who is "quiet" actually is reflective, judicious, unassuming, even-tempered, self-sufficient, and self-effacing, as well as intelligent and eloquent.

Ramesses II, King. Third king of Dynasty XIX. Reigned ca. 1279–1213 B.C. Inveterate builder and husband of Queen Nefertari.

Ramesside Period. The latter portion of the New Kingdom comprising Dynasties XIX–XX (ca. 1292–1070 B.C.). So named from the eleven kings named "Ramesses."

Rê. The great creator god and sun god of Heliopolis.

Red Crown. The royal crown representing dominion over Lower Egypt. Sometimes personified as a goddess.

Rensi. The Lord High Steward to King Nebkaure Khety III of Dynasty X (twenty-first century B.C.) who listens to the complaints of the Eloquent Peasant.

Residence. The. Usual designation for the royal capital.

River, The. Always the Nile, the only actual river in Egypt.

Ro-geese. A species of goose.

Rosetau. Place name denoting "the opening of the paths," the gateway to the realm of the dead. The necropolis.

Royal Friend. An honorific title given by a king to specially favored courtiers, like Sinuhe.

Sakhmet. "The Powerful One." The lioness goddess of Memphis, daughter of Rê and wife of Ptah. She is goddess of war and sickness, plague and destruction.

Saqqara (Sakkara). Along with Giza, the main burial ground for Memphis. One of the greatest archaeological sites in the world, particularly rich in tombs of the Thinite and Old Kingdom periods.

Satire on the Trades. Alternative title of the Middle Kingdom *Instruction for Little Pepi* written by Khety, one of the classic authors of ancient Egypt.

Scribe. The ancient Egyptian writer, usually a professional bureaucrat or lower-level official. But the scribal schools, like that at Deir el-Medineh, are famous for teaching the young their letters and introducing them to the classic literature of ancient Egypt.

Sedge. The reed-like plant used as an emblem of Upper Egypt. See also "He of the Sedge and the Bee."

Sehetepibrê, King. The prenomen of King Amenemhat I (1976–1947 B.C.), first king of Dynasty XII.

Seizer-of-Scalp-Locks; He-of-the-Upreared-Head; Chief-over-Blood-Rites; Traveler; the Bloody-Eyed. All names of minor deities in the other world who hunt down, kill, and process the bodies of the enemies of King Unis.

Sekhet Hetepu. The dwelling of the blessed dead. See also "Field of Reeds."

Sekhet Iaru. See "Field of Reeds."

Sembaq City. Locale in the western Delta.

Semseru. A deity allied to Sopedu.

Senmut. Fort at the first cataract of the Nile in the south of Egypt, near modern Aswan.

Senusert I, King. Second king of Dynasty XII. Reigned 1956–1910 B.C.

Serpent, The. The royal uraeus on the king's brow, and a goddess whose function was to protect the king from his enemies. Also known as "The Eye of Rê."

Seth. The great antagonist god in the Osirian legends, brother (and murderer) of Osiris, uncle of Horus, whose kingdom he tried to usurp. He is also the mythological embodiment of bad character, brute strength, and disruptiveness. Actually, the figure of Seth is more complex than this; and as god of the sterile deserts or in other legends, he is the equal, helper, and companion of Horus.

Shetyt. The precinct of Sokar, god of the Memphite necropolis.

Shu. The god of air in the Heliopolitan theogony, son of Atum (or Rê) and consort of Tefnut, the moisture.

Sinai. The desert region east of Egypt across the Red Sea. In pharaonic times, a mining region and site of major copper mines.

Sinuhe. Title character of one of the finest literary pieces to survive from ancient Egypt. His *Tale* is presented as if it were a tomb-biography of a courtier living in Dynasty XII during the reigns of Amenemhat I and Senusert I. His account presents him as an intimate in the retinue of Queen Neferu and her children. Historical evidence for the existence of Sinuhe has not yet come to light.

Sistrum (pl. sistra). A hand-held rattle-like percussion instrument. The nearest modern equivalents are the castanets and the tambourine.

Skyship. See Barque of Rê.

Sneferu, King. First king of Dynasty IV (ca. 2614–2479 B.C.). *The Prophecy of Neferty* is set at his court.

Sneferu's Island. A locale in Egypt, presumably near Sneferu's pyramid, in Sinuhe's flight into exile in Syria-Palestine.

Sobek. Crocodile god connected with royal power and particularly worshipped in the Fayyum. Son of Neith.

Sobek-Rê. Fusion of the god Sobek with the power and concept of the more venerable god Rê.

Son of the Northwind. Teasing mispronunciation (*Sa-mehyt*) of Sinuhe's name by the royal princesses. See next entry.

Son of the Sycamore. Literal translation of Sinuhe's name (*Sa-nehet*).

Sopdu. Star god and lord of the eastern deserts and the turquoise mines in Sinai.

Soul-priest. The priest responsible for the well-being of the deceased.

Southland, The. The Valley of the Nile south of Cairo, Upper Egypt.

Spell. To us, a "magical" saying; but to the Egyptians a recitation that invoked super-natural power in order to accomplish some desired human purpose.

Sphinx. Royal figure with the head of a king and the body of a lion, betokening royal power. *The* Sphinx lies at Giza in front of the pyramid of King Khaefre (2547–2521 B.C., Dynasty IV) and represents his figure. The Egyptian sphinx is not to be confused with the Greek sphinx.

Staircase of Fire. In the Otherworld, presumably the stairway leading up to the presence of Rê.

Stela (pl. stelae). A stone or slab, set upright and inscribed and/or carved to commemorate a person (i.e., a gravestone), or an event, such as a military victory (a historical stela).

Strabo. First-century B.C. Greek historian and geographer. Egypt is discussed in the final book of his *Geography.*

Sumero-Akkadian literature. Collective term for the literature of the first civilizations of the Tigris-Euphrates River valley: Sumer, on present evidence, the earliest known literate civilization anywhere (end of the fourth millennium B.C.), and Akkad, which challenged and succeeded it.

Sun. Sometimes the physical disk, but usually referring to one of the sun and creator gods, most often, Rê.

Sunfolk. Term for the blessed dead as they are conceived as travelling with the sun in its journey across the heavens. A concept from the sky religion of Rê as opposed to the earth-religion centering on Osiris.

Sycamore. The fig tree prized for its shade but also seen as a tree-goddess, perhaps Hathor, sometimes Nut. Sinuhe is "Son of the Sycamore" but his name might be translated, "Son belonging to the Sycamore-goddess."

Syria-Palestine. Common collective name for the lands of the eastern Mediterranean now comprising Syria, Lebanon, and Israel.

Taiyt. Goddess of weaving, especially of the cloth for embalming.

Tales. One of the major genres of ancient Egyptian literature. The modern term would be "fiction." The Tales range from the very unassuming to the highly sophisticated. Closely associated in form with the tale is myth.

Ta-Mery. "The Beloved Land," that is, Egypt.

Ta-Sety. Southernmost nome of Egypt proper. Often used more generally for the South-land.

Ta-tenen. "Land-rising." The god who represents the emergence of the fertilized land from the waters of the inundation or the first hill of creation from the original chaos. Located at Memphis, he was assimilated into Ptah.

Taweseret. Wife of Amenemopet.

Tefnut. The goddess of moisture, in the Heliopolitan cosmogony, daughter of the creator god and consort of Shu.

Teti, King. (2322–2312 B.C.). First king of Dynasty VI in the Old Kingdom. Represented by a pyramid at Saqqara.

Thebes. The greatest city in ancient Egypt, but perhaps sharing that honor with Memphis. Religious capital of Egypt, possibly from the Middle Kingdom on but certainly so during the New Kingdom and later. Not to be confused with the Greek Thebes of Oedipus.

Thinis (This). Capital city of Egypt during the first two (Thinite) dynasties. Near Abydos.

Thirty, The. Local deliberative and judicial body of officials.

Thomas, Dylan. Welsh poet (1914–1953).

Thoth. The god of wisdom, writing, the sacred books, scribes, and intellectual and literary achievement in general.

Thought Couplets. The structuring device of most ancient Egyptian poetry. The verse lines occur in pairs, each line comprised of (usually) one clause, either dependent or independent, and the pair making up the full sentence and the complete thought.

Titulary (Royal). Term for the formal series of five great names for the Egyptian pharaoh, consisting of (1) the Horus name, symbolizing the king's relationship to the cosmic falcon god; (2) the Two Ladies name (*nebty*) expressing his connection with the two most important goddesses of Upper and Lower Egypt at the beginning of Dynasty I, the vulture-goddess Nekhbet and the cobra-goddess Edjo, respectively; (3) the Horus of Gold name, the significance of which is not clear; (4) the prenomen (*n-sw-bity;* "He of the Sedge and the Bee"), which expresses his relationship to the symbolic plant of Upper Egypt and the symbolic animal of Lower Egypt; and (5) the nomen ("Son of Rê"), which signifies his kinship with the sun god. It is the last two of these that are most common and are enclosed in cartouches.

Tura. Site of quarries for fine limestone since the Old Kingdom. Near Cairo.

Tutankhamun, King. Reigned 1333–1323 B.C. The boy-king whose mummy and virtually intact funerary treasure were discovered in 1922 by Howard Carter, just one century after Champollion deciphered the hieroglyphs.

Twin Lands. See Two Lands.

Two Conclaves of gods. The Greater and Lesser Enneads.

Two Fish Canal. Southern border of the Western Delta.

Two Ladies, The. The second, or *nebty,* name in the royal titulary, signifying the king's rule of the united Two Lands under the symbols of their tutelary goddesses: Nekhbet, the vulture-goddess of Upper Egypt, and Wadjet, the snake-goddess of Lower Egypt.

Two Lands, The. A common name for Egypt as the union of two originally separate lands.

Two Mighty Ones, The. Presumably Horus and Seth (from the context in *The Prophecy of Neferty*).

Two Phoenicians Coastlands, The. In *Sinuhe,* term for the lands of the "*Fenekhu*" as of the twentieth century B.C. and presumably the ancestors of those who became known to history as the Phoenicians.

Two Shores, The. Another common name for Egypt, emphasizing the eastern and western banks of the Nile.

Underworld. The place of the afterlife according to ancient Egyptian religion. For all who passed the Final Judgment by Osiris, it meant a life of happiness, fulfillment, and ease, eternally in the presence of god.

Upper Egypt. Southern Egypt, the River Valley.

Upper Retenu. Locale in Syria-Palestine where Sinuhe spent most of his life in exile. Ruled by Prince Amunenshi and containing the district of Yaa, the land given to Sinuhe by the Prince.

Uraeus (pl. uraei). Figurine of serpent attached to crown. See "The Serpent." See also "The Eye of Rê."

Ur-god. Designation for the original, primal god of creation in the beginning, called by various names at different times, but generally known as Atum.

Ur-waters. The original or primordial watery waste before creation of the universe.

Valley of the Kings. The royal necropolis in western Thebes during the New Kingdom.

Vizier. The highest official in the Egyptian state under the king. He was charged with upholding justice and had complete control over all the country's administrative machinery.

Walls-of-the-Ruler. A fort at the northeastern border of Egypt, built by Amenemhat I of Dynasty XII to ward off and control Asiatic nomads. Skirted by Sinuhe in his flight to Syria-Palestine.

Wawat. The northernmost region of Nubia at the border with Egypt.

Weary-hearted, The. Designation for the murdered Osiris, inert and weary in death prior to his resurrection.

West, The. Symbolic name for the region of the dead. To go to the West means to die. The idea included the final crossing of the Nile to the burial ground on the west bank. It also meant a happy and vigorous Afterlife.

Western Land. See previous entry.

Western Mountains. The area where the sun sets; symbolically, the place of the Afterlife.

White Crown. The crown of Upper Egypt, sometimes personified as a goddess.

Whitman, Walt. American poet (1819–1892).

Wisdom Texts. A common name for a variety of didactic or admonitory literary works intended to pass on one's wisdom and experience to the next generation.

Word of God. The sacred writings of ancient Egypt written in the sacred language (the hieroglyphs or hieratic). They were not canonized into a single scripture but recorded those moments when a god spoke to human beings.

Yaa. The district of Upper Retenu given to Sinuhe as a wedding gift by Amunenshi.

Yahwist, The. The earliest writer whose hand is visible in composition of the Pentateuch. A southerner (Judean) who perhaps lived at court during the United Monarchy (the Third Intermediate Period) and wrote ca. 950 B.C.

LIST OF HIEROGLYPHIC PASSAGES

SOURCES OF THE TEXTS

Akhenaten's *Hymn to the Sun*

Norman de Garis Davies, *The Rock Tombs of el Amarna*, Vol. 6, Archeological Survey of Egypt, Eighteenth Memoir (London: Egypt Exploration Fund, 1907; reprint 1975), pl. 27.

The Tale of the Shipwrecked Sailor

Pap. Leningrad 1115. In V.S. Golénischchev, *Les papyrus hiératique nos. 1115, 1116A, et 1116B de l'Hermitage Impérial à St. Petersburg* (St. Petersburg, 1913). Transcription: Aylward M. Blackman, *Middle Egyptian Stories*, pt. 1, Bibliotheca Aegyptiaca 2 (Brussels: La Fondation Égyptologique Reine Élisabeth, 1931), pp. 41–48.

"Why, just now, must you question your heart"

Pap. Chester Beatty I, recto 17.3–4. In Bernard Mathieu, *La Poésie amoureuse de l'Égypte ancienne*, Bibliothéque d'Étude 115 (Cairo: Institut Français d'Archéologie Orientale, 1996), pl. 7.

"I love you through the daytimes"

Cairo Ostracon 25218, augmented by Ostracon Deir el-Medineh 1266, lines 1–3. In Bernard Mathieu, *La Poésie amoureuse de l'Égypte ancienne*, Bibliothéque d'Étude 115 (Cairo: Institut Français d'Archéologie Orientale, 1996), pl. 17.

"My love is one and only"

Pap. Chester Beatty I, verso C1.1–8. In Bernard Mathieu, *La Poésie amoureuse de l'Égypte ancienne*, Bibliothéque d'Étude 115 (Cairo: Institut Français d'Archéologie Orientale, 1996), pl. 1.

"Love, how I'd love to slip down to the pond"

Cairo Ostracon 25218, augmented by Ostracon Deir el-Medineh 1266, lines 8–11. In Bernard Mathieu, *La Poésie amoureuse de l'Égypte ancienne,* Bibliothèque d'Étude 115 (Cairo: Institut Français d'Archéologie Orientale, 1996), pl. 18.

"Love of you is mixed deep in my vitals"

Pap. Harris 500, recto 1.6–10. In Bernard Mathieu, *La Poésie amoureuse de l'Égypte ancienne,* Bibliothèque d'Étude 115 (Cairo: Institut Français d'Archéologie Orientale, 1996), pl. 8.

"I think I'll go home and lie very still"

Pap. Harris 500, recto 2.9–11. In Bernard Mathieu, *La Poésie amoureuse de l'Égypte ancienne,* Bibliothèque d'Étude 115 (Cairo: Institut Français d'Archéologie Orientale, 1996), pl. 9.

Songs of the Birdcatcher's Daughter

Pap. Harris 500, recto 4.1–6.2. In Bernard Mathieu, *La Poésie amoureuse de l'Égypte ancienne,* Bibliothèque d'Étude 115 (Cairo: Institut Français d'Archéologie Orientale, 1996), pls. 11–13.

The Instruction for Little Pepi

W. Helck, *Die Lehre des Dw3-Ḥtjj,* 2 parts (Wiesbaden: Otto Harrassowitz, 1970). In addition, Georges Posener, *Catalogue des Ostraca Hiératiques Littéraire de Deir el Médineh,* Tome III (Publications de l'Institut Français d'Archéologie Orientale: Cairo, 1977–1980).

Longing for Memphis

Pap. Anastasi IV, 4.10–5.5. In Alan H. Gardiner, *Late-Egyptian Miscellanies,* Bibliotheca Aegyptiaca VII (Brussels: La Fondation Égyptologique Reine Élisabeth, 1937), p. 39.

"Oh, I'm bound downstream on the Memphis Ferry"

Pap. Harris 500, recto 2.5–9. In Bernard Mathieu, *La Poésie amoureuse de l'Égypte ancienne,* Bibliothèque d'Étude 115 (Cairo: Institut Français d'Archéologie Orientale, 1996), pl. 9.

Rebuke Addressed to a Dissipated Scribe

Pap. Anastasi IV, 11.8–12.5. Text in Alan.H. Gardiner, *Late-Egyptian Miscellanies,* Bibliotheca Aegyptiaca VII (Brussels: La Fondation Égyptologique Reine Élisabeth, 1937), pp. 47–48.

Menna's Lament

Oriental Institute Chicago Ostracon 12074. Translated directly from the ostracon. Facsimile and transcription in Jaroslav Černý and Alan H. Gardiner, *Hieratic Ostraca,* vol. 1 (Oxford: Griffith Institute, 1957) pls. 78–79a.

The Debate between a Man Tired of Life and His Soul

Pap. Berlin 3024. Hieratic text best read in Hans Goedicke, *The Report about the Dispute of a Man with His Ba* (Baltimore: The Johns Hopkins Press, 1970).

The Resurrection of King Unis

Tomb of Unis: Utterances 273–274. In Kurt Sethe, ed., *Die Altägyptischen Pyramidentexte,* vol. 1 (Leipzig: J. C. Hinrichs, 1908; reprint: Hildesheim: Georg Olms), 1969, pp. 205–216).

Prayer to the King to Rise Up

Pyramid Text 373. In Kurt Sethe, ed., *Die Altägyptischen Pyramidentexte,* vol. 1 (Leipzig: J. C. Hinrichs, 1908; reprint: Hildesheim: Georg Olms, 1969), pp. 358–362.

Hymn to the King as a Primordial God

Pyramid Text 486. In Kurt Sethe, ed., *Die Altägyptischen Pyramidentexte, vol. 2* (Leipzig: J. C. Hinrichs, 1908; reprint: Hildesheim: Georg Olms, 1969), pp. 80–83.

Hymn to the King as a Flash of Lightning

Pyramid Text 261. In Kurt Sethe, ed., *Die Altägyptischen Pyramidentexte, vol. 1* (Leipzig: J. C. Hinrichs, 1908; reprint: Hildesheim: Georg Olms, 1969), pp. 174–175.

Prayer of the King as a Star Fading in the Dawn

Pyramid Text 216. In Kurt Sethe, ed., *Die Altägyptischen Pyramidentexte, vol. 1* (Leipzig: J. C. Hinrichs, 1908; reprint: Hildesheim: Georg Olms, 1969), pp. 85–86.

The Prophecy of Neferty

Papyrus Petersburg 1116B. In V.S. Golénischchev, *Les papyrus hiératique nos. 1115, 1116A, et 1116B de l'Hermitage Impériale à St. Petersburg* (St. Petersburg, 1913). Best read, with the parallel texts, in Wolfgang Helck, *Die Prophezeiung des Nfr.tj,* 2nd ed. (Wiesbaden: Otto Harrassowitz, 1992).

The Testament of Amenemhat

In Jesús López, "Le Papyrus Millingen," *Revue d'égyptologie* 15 (1963), 29–33 and pls. 4–8, as well as many other papyri and ostraca. Fullest transcription in Wolfgang Helck, "Der Text der 'Lehre Amenemhats I. Für seinen Sohn,'" *Kleine Ägyptische Texte* (Wiesbaden: Otto Harrassowitz, 1969). Also, John Foster, "The Conclusion to 'The Testament of Ammenemes, King of Egypt,'" *Journal of Egyptian Archaeology* 67 (1981), 36–47 and pls. 4–11.

Two Spells

Spell for Causing the Beloved to Follow After: Deir el-Medineh Ostracon 1057. In Georges Posener, *Catalogue des ostraca hiératique littéraire de Deir el Médineh,* tome 1 (Cairo: L'Institut Français d'Archéologie Orientale, 1938), pls. 31–31a.

Power from the Four Winds of Heaven: Coffin Texts, Spell 162. In Adriaan de Buck, *The Egyptian Coffin Texts,* vol. 2 (Chicago: University of Chicago Press, 1938), pp. 389–405.

The Greatness of the King

Pap. Kahun LV.1. In Francis Llewellyn Griffith, *The Petrie Papyri: Hieratic Papyri from Kahun and Gurob (Principally of the Middle Kingdom),* (London: B. Quaritch, 1898).

Prayer of King Ramesses II

K. A. Kitchen, *Ramesside Inscriptions Historical and Biographical,* vol. II (Oxford: Blackwell, 1979), pp. 34–44.

For a Portrait of the Queen

Luxor Temple, Court of Ramesses II, West Wall, North of Doorway. Cf. Bertha Porter and Rosalind L. B. Moss, *Topographical Bibliography of Ancient Egyptian Hieroglyphic Texts, Reliefs, and Paintings: Theban Temples,* Vol. 2, 2nd ed. (Oxford: Clarendon Press, 1972), p. 308 (a28: III). Text taken from translator's hand copy.

Hymn to Osiris

Stele of Amenmose, Louvre C. 286. In Alexandre Moret, "La légend d'Osiris," *Bulletin de l'Institut Français d'Archéologie Orientale* 30 (1931), 725–30 and pl. 1–3.

Hymn to the Nile

Papyri Turin 1968 + 1878 + 1890, Pap. Anastasi VII, Pap. Chester Beatty V, Pap. Sallier II, and numerous ostraca. Best read in Dirk Van der Plas, *L'Hymne à la Crue du Nil,* 2 vols (Leiden: Nederlands Instituut voor het Nabije Oosten, 1986).

Hymn to the Rising Sun

Papyrus of Ani, Ch. XV. In E. A. Wallis Budge, *The Chapters of Coming Forth by Day . . . ,* vol. I (London: Kegan Paul, Trench, Trübner & Co., 1910), pp.36–38.

In Praise of Amun

Pap. Anastasi II. In Alan H. Gardiner, *Late-Egyptian Miscellanies,* Bibliotheca Aegyptiaca VII (Brussels: La Fondation Égyptologique Reine Élisabeth, 1937), pp. 17–18.

Lament to Amun

Pap. Anastasi IV, 10.1–5. In Alan H. Gardiner, *Late-Egyptian Miscellanies* (Brussels: La Fondation Égyptologique Reine Élisabeth, 1937), p. 39.

The Tale of Sinuhe

Pap. Berlin 3022 and 10499, Ashmolean Ostracon of *Sinuhe,* and several fragmentary ostraca and pieces of papyrus. Cf. Alan H. Gardiner, *Die Erzählung des Sinuhe und Die Hirtengeschichte, Literarische Texte des Mittleren Reiches* 2. Vol. 5 *Hieratische Papyrus aus den Königlichen Museen zu Berlin* (Leipzig: J. Hinrichs, 1909; reprint 1970). Also: J. Barns, *The Ashmolean Ostracon of Sinuhe* (Oxford: Griffith Institute, 1952). A parallel text transcription in Roland Koch, *Die Erzählung des Sinuhe,* Bibliotheca Aegyptiaca XVII (Brussels: La Fondation Égyptologique Reine Élisabeth, 1990).

From *The Leiden Hymns*

Pap. Leiden I 350. Transcription in Jan Zandee, *De Hymnen aan Amon van Papyrus Leiden I 350* (Leiden: Rijksmuseum van Oudheden, 1947), esp. Bijlage 1, "Hieroglyphische Tekst," pls. 1–6.

The Prayers of Pahery

From the tomb of Paheri at el-Kab. Text in J. J. Tylor and Francis Llewellyn Griffith, *The Tomb of Paheri at El Kab,* Eleventh Memoir (London: The Egypt Exploration Fund, 1894), pl. IX. Also, Kurt Sethe, *Urkunden der 18. Dynastie,* Urkunden des ägyptisches

Altertums IV. 2nd ed. (Berlin: Akademie-Verlag, 1927–1930; reprinted 1961), I.111–123.

From the Tomb of King Intef

Pap. Harris 500, recto 6.3–7.3. In Michael V. Fox, *The Song of Songs and the Ancient Egyptian Love Songs* (Madison: University of Wisconsin Press, 1985), pp.378–380.

The Harper's Song for Inherkhawy

Deir el-Medineh Tomb 359, Wall 11, Register 3, Scene 17. Facsimile in Bernard Bruyère, *Fouilles de l'Institut Français d'Archéologie Orientale* 8 (Cairo: L'Institut Français d'Archéologie Orientale, 1930), p. 70 and pl. 23.

From *The Eloquent Peasant*

Pap. Berlin 3023, 3025 and 10499, and Pap. British Museum 10274. Parallel text edition in R. B. Parkinson, *The Tale of the Eloquent Peasant* (Oxford: Griffith Institute, 1991).

From *The Maxims of Ptahhotep*

Pap. Prisse and others. Facsimile: G. Jéquier, *Le papyrus Prisse et ses variantes* (Paris, 1911). Transcription of the main papyri: Z. Žaba, *Les maximes de Ptahhotep* (Prague, 1956), esp. pp. 15–21.

The Instruction for Merikarê

Pap. Petersburg 1116A. In V. S. Golénischchev, *Les Papyrus hiératique nos. 1115, 1116A, and 1116B de l'Hermitage Impériale à St. Pétersbourg* (St. Petersburg, 1913), pls. 9–14.

The Wisdom of Amenemopet

Pap. British Museum 10474. Transcription in H. O. Lange, *Das Weisheitsbuch des Amenemope* (Copenhagen: A. F. Hoest & Son, 1925).

The Immortality of Writers (Epilogue)

Pap. Chester Beatty IV (= Pap. British Museum 10684), verso II.5–III.10. In Alan H. Gardiner, *Hieratic Papyri in the British Museum,* 3rd series, II (London: British Museum, 1935), pls. 18–19.

BIBLIOGRAPHY

Aldred, Cyril

1980   *Egyptian Art.* New York: Oxford University Press.

1987   *The Egyptians.* New York: Thames & Hudson.

1988   *Akhenaten: King of Egypt.* London: Thames & Hudson.

Allen, James

2000   *Middle Egyptian: An Introduction to the Language and Culture of Hieroglyphs.*
            Cambridge: Cambridge University Press.

Allen, Thomas George

1960   *The Egyptian Book of the Dead: Documents in the Oriental Institute Museum at
            the University of Chicago.* Oriental Institute Publications 82. Chicago:
            University of Chicago Press.

Arnold, Dieter

1991   *Building in Egypt: Pharaonic Stone Masonry.* New York: Oxford University
            Press.

Assmann, Jan

1995   *Egyptian Solar Religion: Re, Amun and the Crisis of Polytheism.* Translated by
            Anthony Alcock. London and New York: Kegan Paul International.

1999   *Ägyptische Hymnen und Gebete.* 2nd ed. Ophis Biblienset Orientalis:
            Freiburg and Göttinger.

Badawy, Alexander

1954–68   *A History of Egyptian Architecture.* 3 vols. Berkeley: University of California
            Press.

Baines, John, and Jaromír Málek
1980   *Atlas of Ancient Egypt.* London: Phaidon Press.

Barucq, André, and François Daumas
1980   *Hymnes et Prieres de l'Égypte Ancienne.* Littératures Anciennes du
        Proche-Orient. Paris: Cerf.

Bierbriar, Morris
1982   *The Tomb-Builders of the Pharaohs.* London: British Museum.

Blackman, Aylward M.
1931   *Middle Egyptian Stories,* pt. 1, Bibliotheca Aegyptiaca 2. Brussels: La
        Fondation Égyptologique Reine Élisabeth.

Bowman, Alan K.
1986   *Egypt after the Pharaohs: 332 B.C.–642 A.D.* University of California Press.

Bruyére, Bernard
1930   *Fouilles de l'Institut Français d'Archéologie Orientale.* VIII, fasc. iii, Plates
        XXII,3 and XXIII, p. 70. Cairo: Institut Français d'Archéologie Orientale.

Buck, Adriaan de
1938   *The Egyptian Coffin Texts.* Vol. 2. Chicago: University of Chicago Press.
1963   *Egyptian Readingbook.* Leiden: Nederlands Instituut voor het Nabije
        Oosten.

Budge, E. A. Wallis
1910   *The Chapters of Coming Forth by Day or the Theban Recension of the Book of the
        Dead. The Egyptian Hieroglyphic Text Edited from Numerous Papyri.* 4 vols.
        (with vocabulary). Books on Egypt and Chaldea. London: Kegan Paul,
        Trench, Trübner. [Reprinted AMS Press, 1976.]

Caminos, Ricardo A.
1954   *Late-Egyptian Miscellanies.* London: Oxford University Press.

Černý, Jaroslav, and Alan Gardiner
1957   *Hieratic Ostraca.* Oxford: Oxford University Press.

David, Rosalie
1986   *The Pyramid Builders of Ancient Egypt.* London: Routledge & Kegan Paul.

Davies, Norman de Garis

1908   *The Rock Tombs of el Amarna. Vol. VI. — Tombs of Parennefer, Tutu, and Aÿ.*
        Archeological Survey of Egypt, Eighteenth Memoir. London: Egypt
        Exploration Fund. [Reprinted 1975]

1953   *The Temple of Hibis III.* New York: Metropolitan Museum of Art Egyptian
        Expedition.

Edwards, Amelia B.

1877   *A Thousand Miles up the Nile.* London: Longmans, Green & Co. [Reprint
        1982]

Edwards, I. E. S.

1939   *Hieroglyphic Texts from Egyptian Stelae, etc.* Vol. 8. London: British Museum.

1986   *The Pyramids of Egypt.* Rev. ed. New York: Viking Penguin.

Edwards, I. E. S., C. J. Gadd, and N. G. L. Hammond, eds.

1970–75 *The Cambridge Ancient History.* 3rd ed. Vols. I–II. Cambridge: Cambridge
        University Press.

Emery, Walter B.

1961   *Archaic Egypt.* Baltimore: Penguin Books.

Epigraphic Survey, The

1980   *The Tomb of Kheruef: Theban Tomb 192.* Oriental Institute Publications 102.
        Chicago: The Oriental Institute of the University of Chicago.

Erichsen, Wolja

1933   *Papyrus Harris I: Hieroglyphische Transkription.* Bibliotheca Aegyptiaca V.
        Brussels: La Fondation Égyptologique Reine Élisabeth.

Erman, Adolf

1927   *The Ancient Egyptians: A Sourcebook of Their Writings.* Translated by
        Aylward M. Blackman. New York: Harper & Row. [Introduction to the
        Torchbook edition, 1966, by William Kelly Simpson]

Erman, Adolf, and Hermann Grapow, eds.

1926–31 *Wörterbuch der ägyptischen Sprache.* 7 vols. Leipzig: J. C. Hinrichs.
        [Reprinted 1971]

Faulkner, Raymond O.

1962   *A Concise Dictionary of Middle Egyptian.* Oxford: Griffith Institute.

1969   *The Ancient Egyptian Pyramid Texts.* Oxford: Oxford University Press.

1973–78   *The Ancient Egyptian Coffin Texts.* 3 vols. Warminster, England: Aris & Phillips.

1985   *The Ancient Egyptian Book of the Dead.* Rev. ed. Edited by Carol Andrews. New York: Macmillan.

Fischer-Elfert, Hans-Werner

1986   *Literarische Ostraka der Ramessidenzeit in Übersetzung.* Kleine Ägyptische Texte. Wiesbaden: Otto Harrassowitz.

Foster, John L.

1974   *Love Songs of the New Kingdom.* New York: Charles Scribner's Sons. [Reprinted University of Texas Press, 1992]

1981   "The Conclusion to 'The Testament of Ammenemes, King of Egypt,'" *Journal of Egyptian Archaeology* 67: 36–47 and pls. 4–11.

1988   " 'The Shipwrecked Sailor': Prose or Verse? (Postponing Clauses and Tense Neutral Clauses)," *Studien zur altägyptische Kultur* 15: 69–109.

1992   *Echoes of Egyptian Voices: An Anthology of Ancient Egyptian Poetry.* Norman and London: University of Oklahoma Press.

1993   *Thought Couplets in The Tale of Sinuhe.* Münchener Ägyptologische Untersuchungen 3. Frankfurt: Verlag Peter Lang.

1995   *Hymns, Prayers, and Songs: An Anthology of Ancient Egyptian Lyric Poetry.* SBL Writings from the Ancient World 8. Atlanta: Scholars Press.

Fox, Michael V.

1985   *The Song of Songs and the Ancient Egyptian Love Songs.* Madison: University of Wisconsin Press.

Freed, Rita

1987   *Ramesses the Great: His Life and World.* Memphis: City of Memphis, TN.

Gardiner, Alan H.

1931   *The Library of A. Chester Beatty: Description of a Hieratic Papyrus with a Mythological Story, Love-Songs, and Other Miscellaneous Texts.* Oxford: Oxford University Press.

1935   *Hieratic Papyri in the British Museum.* 3rd series, Vol. II. London: British Museum.

1937   *Late-Egyptian Miscellanies.* Bibliotheca Aegyptiaca VII. Brussels: La Fondation Égyptologique Reine Élisabeth.
1957   *Egyptian Grammar.* 3rd ed. Oxford: Griffith Institute.
1961   *Egypt of the Pharaohs.* Oxford: Oxford University Press.

Gilbert, Pierre
1949   *La Poésie Égyptienne.* 2nd ed. Brussels: La Fondation Égyptologique Reine Élisabeth.

Goedicke, Hans
1970   *The Report about the Dispute of a Man with His Ba.* Baltimore: The Johns Hopkins Press.

Golénischchev, V. S.
1913   *Les Papyrus hiératique nos. 1115, 1116A, and 1116B de l'Hermitage Impériale à St. Pétersbourg.* St. Petersburg: n.p.
1927   *Papyrus Hiératiques.* Catalogue général des antiquités Égyptiennes du Musée Caire, Nos. 58001–58036. Cairo: Institut Français d'Archéologie Orientale.

Griffith, Francis Llewellyn
1898   *The Petrie Papyri. Hieratic Papyri from Kahun and Gurob (Principally of the Middle Kingdom).* London: B. Quaritch.

Grimal, Nicholas
1992   *A History of Ancient Egypt.* Translated by Ian Shaw. Oxford: Blackwell.

Hari, Robert
1985   *La Tombe Thébaine du Père Divin Neferhotep (TT50).* Geneva: Éditions de Belles-Lettres.

Harpur, Yvonne
1987   *Decoration in Egyptian Tombs of the Old Kingdom.* London: KPI.

Harris, J. R., ed.
1971   *The Legacy of Egypt.* 2nd ed. Oxford: Clarendon Press.

Hart, George
1986   *A Dictionary of Egyptian Gods and Goddesses.* London: Routledge & Kegan Paul.

Hayes, William C.
1953   *The Scepter of Egypt*. Rev. ed. 2 vols. New York: Metropolitan Museum of
          Art.

Helck, Wolfgang
1955–58   *Urkunden der 18. Dynastie, Hefte 20–22*. Berlin: Akademie-Verlag.
1969   "Der Text der 'Lehre Amenemhats I. Für seinen Sohn.' " In *Kleine
          Ägyptische Texte*. Wiesbaden: Otto Harrassowitz.
1992   *Die Prophezeiung des Nfr.tj*, 2nd ed. Wiesbaden: Otto Harrassowitz.

Helck, Wolfgang, and Eberhard Otto, eds.
1975–92   *Lexikon der Ägyptologie*. 7 vols. Wiesbaden: Otto Harrassowitz.

Hermann, Alfred
1959   *Altägyptische Liebesdichtung*. Wiesbaden: Otto Harrassowitz.

Hoffman, Michael A.
1979   *Egypt before the Pharaohs*. New York: Knopf.

Hornung, Erik
1982   *Conceptions of God in Ancient Egypt: The One and the Many*. Translated by
          John Baines. Ithaca, New York: Cornell University Press.
1990   *The Valley of the Kings: Horizon of Eternity*. New York: Timken.
1992   *Idea into Image: Essays on Ancient Egyptian Thought*. Translated by Elizabeth
          Bredeck. New York: Timken.
1999   *Akhenaten and the Religion of Light*. Translated by David Lorton. Ithaca,
          New York: Cornell University Press.

Hovedstreydt, W., L. M. J. Zonhoven, et al.
1947   *Annual Egyptological Bibliography*; Leiden: Nederlands Instituut voor het
          Nabije Oosten. [Complete through 1997]

James, T. G. H.
1979   *An Introduction to Ancient Egypt*. New York: Farrar, Straus & Giroux.
1984   *Pharaoh's People: Scenes from Life in Imperial Egypt*. Chicago: University of
          Chicago Press.

Jéquier, G.
1911   *Le papyrus Prisse et ses variantes*. Paris: n.p.

Kemp, Barry J.

1989   *Ancient Egypt: Anatomy of a Civilization.* London: Routledge.

Kitchen, K. A.

1975–90   *Ramesside Inscriptions Historical and Biographical.* 8 vols. Oxford: Blackwell.

1982   *Pharaoh Triumphant: The Life and Times of Ramesses II.* Warminster, England: Aris & Phillips.

1999   *Poetry of Ancient Egypt.* Jonsered, Sweden: Paul Åstrom.

Lange, H. O.

1925   *Das Weisheitsbuch des Amenemope.* Copenhagen: A. F. Hoest & Son.

Lange, Kurt, and Max Hirmer

1968   *Egypt: Architecture, Sculpture, Painting.* 4th ed. Translated by R. H. Boothroyd. London: Phaidon.

Lauer, Jean-Phillipe

1976   *Saqqara: The Royal Cemetery of Memphis.* New York: Charles Scribner's Sons.

Lichtheim, Miriam

1945   "The Songs of the Harpers," *Journal of Near Eastern Studies* 4: 178–212 and pls. 1–7.

1973–80   *Ancient Egyptian Literature.* 3 vols. Berkeley: University of California Press.

López, Jesús

1963   "Le Papyrus Millingen," *Revue d'égyptologie* 15: 29–33 and pls. 4–8.

Loprieno, Antonio

1995   *Ancient Egyptian: A Linguistic Introduction.* Cambridge: Cambridge University Press.

Loprieno, Antonio, ed.

1996   *Ancient Egyptian Literature: History & Forms.* Leiden, Netherlands: Brill.

Manniche, Lise

1987   *City of the Dead: Thebes in Egypt.* Chicago: University of Chicago Press.

Mariette, Auguste

1872   *Les Papyrus Égyptiennes du Musée Boulaq* II. Paris: A. Franck.

Martin, Geoffrey Thorndike

1989   *The Memphite Tomb of Horemheb Commander-in-Chief of Tut'ankhamun.I: The Reliefs, Inscriptions, and Commentary.* Fifty-Fifth Excavation Memoir. London: Egypt Exploration Society.

1991   *The Hidden Tombs of Memphis.* London: Thames & Hudson.

Mathieu, Bernard

1996   *La Poésie amoureuse de L'Égypte ancienne.* Cairo: Institut Français d'Archéologie Orientale, Bibliothèque d'Étude 115.

Meeks, Dimitri, and Christine Favard-Meeks

1996   *Daily Life of the Egyptian Gods.* Translated from the French by G. M. Goshgarian. Ithaca, New York: Cornell University Press. [Translated from the French original of 1993.]

Mekhitarian, Arpag

1954   *Egyptian Painting.* Geneva: Skira.

Morenz, Siegfried

1973   *Egyptian Religion.* Translated by Ann E. Keep. London: Methuen. [Original edition, 1960.]

Moret, Alexandre

1931   "La légend d'Osiris," *Bulletin de l'Institut Français d'Archéologie Orientale* 30: 725–730 and Plates I–III. Cairo.

Müller, W. M.

1899   *Die Liebespoesie der alten Ägypter.* Leipzig: J. C. Hinrichs.

Murnane, William J.

1995   *Texts from the Amarna Period in Egypt.* SBL Writings from the Ancient World 5. Atlanta: Scholars Press.

Naville, Edouard

1886   *Das Ägyptische Totenbuch der XVIII. bis XX. Dynastie.* 3 vols. Berlin: A. Asher. [Reprinted 1971.]

Nims, Charles F.

1965   *Thebes of the Pharaohs.* New York: Stein & Day.

Parkinson, R. B.
1991   *The Tale of the Eloquent Peasant.* Oxford: Griffith Institute.
1991   *Voices from Ancient Egypt: An Anthology of Middle Kingdom Writings.* Norman: University of Oklahoma Press.
1997   *The Tale of Sinuhe and other Ancient Egyptian Poems, 1940–1640 BC.* Oxford: Clarendon Press.

Peck, William H., and John G. Ross
1978   *Egyptian Drawings.* New York: E. P. Dutton.

Porter, Bertha, and Rosalind L. B. Moss
1972   *Topographical Bibliography of Ancient Egyptian Hieroglyphic Texts, Reliefs, and Paintings: Theban Temples.* Vol. 2, 2nd ed. Oxford: Clarendon Press.

Posener, Georges
1938–80   *Catalogue des Ostraca Hiératiques Littéraires de Deir el Médineh.* 3 vols. Cairo: Institut Français d'Archéologie Orientale.
1971   "Literature." In *The Legacy of Egypt,* J. R. Harris, ed. 2nd ed. Oxford: Oxford University Press. [Chapter 9]

Pritchard, James Bennett
1955   *Ancient Near Eastern Texts Relating to the Old Testament.* 2nd ed. Egyptian texts translated by John A. Wilson. Princeton: Princeton University Press.

Quirke, Stephen
1992   *Ancient Egyptian Religion.* London: British Museum Press.

Redford, Donald B.
1984   *Akhenaten: The Heretic King.* Princeton: Princeton University Press.
1992   *Egypt, Canaan, and Israel in Ancient Times.* Princeton: Princeton University Press.

Redford, Donald B., ed.
2000   *The Oxford Encyclopedia of Ancient Egypt.* 3 vols. New York: Oxford University Press.

Riefstahl, Elizabeth
1964   *Thebes in the Time of Amunhotep III.* Norman: University of Oklahoma Press.

Robins, Gay

1993   *Women in Ancient Egypt.* Cambridge: Harvard University Press.

Romano, James F.

1979   *Catalogue of the Luxor Museum of Ancient Egyptian Art.* Cairo: American
        Research Center in Egypt.

Russman, Edna R.

1989   *Egyptian Sculpture: Cairo and Luxor.* Austin: University of Texas Press.

Sandman, Maj

1938   *Texts from the Time of Akhenaten.* Bibliotheca Aegyptiaca VIII. Brussels: La
        Fondation Égyptologique Reine Élisabeth.

Sasson, Jack M., et. al., eds.

1995   *Civilizations of the Ancient Near East.* 4 vols. New York: Charles Scribner's
        Sons.

Sethe, Kurt

1908   *Die Altägyptischen Pyramidentexte.* 4 vols. Leipzig: J. C. Hinrichs. [Reprinted
        Georg Olms, Hildesheim, 1969]

1927–30 *Urkunden der 18. Dynastie.* Urkunden des ägyptische Altertums IV. 2nd ed.
        4 vols. Berlin: Akademie-Verlag. [Reprinted 1961]

1933   *Urkunden des alten Reichs.* Urkunden des ägyptischen Altertums I. 2nd ed.
        Leipzig: J. C. Hinrichs.

Shafer, Byron E., ed.

1991   *Religion in Ancient Egypt: Gods, Myths, and Personal Practice.* Ithaca, New
        York: Cornell University Press.

Silverman, David P. ed.

1994   *For His Ka: Essays Offered in Memory of Klaus Baer.* Studies in Ancient
        Oriental Civilizations 55. Chicago: Oriental Institute Press.

1997   *Ancient Egypt.* New York: Oxford University Press.

Simpson, William Kelly, Raymond O. Faulkner, and Edward F. Wente, Jr.

1973   *The Literature of Ancient Egypt.* 2nd ed. New Haven, Conn.: Yale University
        Press. [3rd edition forthcoming]

Smith, W. Stevenson, and William Kelly Simpson
1981   *The Art and Architecture of Ancient Egypt.* 2nd ed. The Pelican History of Art.
            New York: Penguin. [Original edition, 1958]

Spencer, A. Jeffrey
1993   *Early Egypt: The Rise of Civilization in the Nile Valley.* London: British
            Museum Press.

Trigger, B. J., B. J. Kemp, D. O'Connor, and A. B. Lloyd
1983   *Ancient Egypt: A Social History.* Cambridge: Cambridge University Press.

Tylor, J. J., and Francis Llewellyn Griffith
1894   *The Tomb of Paheri at El Kab.* Eleventh Memoir. London: Egypt Exploration
            Fund. [Bound with Edouard Naville, *Ahnas el Medineh Heracleopolis Magna.*
            Reprinted 1981.]

Van der Plas, Dirk
1986   *L'Hymne à la Crue du Nil.* 2 vols. Leiden: Nederlands Instituut voor het
            Nabije Oosten.

Weeks, Kent
1998   *The Lost Tomb.* New York: William Morrow.

Wente, Edward F.
1980   Translations in The Epigraphic Survey, *The Tomb of Kheruef: Theban Tomb
            192.* Oriental Institute Publications 102. Chicago: The Oriental Institute
            of the University of Chicago.
1990   *Letters from Ancient Egypt.* SBL Writings from the Ancient World 1.
            Atlanta: Scholars Press.

Wilson, John A.
1951   *The Culture of Ancient Egypt.* Chicago: University of Chicago Press.

Yoyotte, Jean
1968   *Treasures of the Pharaohs.* Geneva: Skira.

Žaba, Z.
1956   *Les maximes de Ptahhotep.* Prague: n.p.

Žabkar, Louis V.

1988   *Hymns to Isis in Her Temple at Philae*. Hanover, New Hampshire: Published for Brandeis University Press by the University Press of New England.

Zandee, Jan

1947   *De Hymnen aan Amon van Papyrus Leiden I 350,* recto. Oudheidkundige Mededelingen uit het Rijksmuseum van Oudheded, New Series XXVIII. Leiden, Netherlands: Het Rijksmuseum van Oudheden.